THE POEMS
OF
SHAKESPEARE'S
DARK LADY

THE POEMS
OF
SHAKESPEARE'S
DARK LADY

Salve Deus Rex Judæorum
by
EMILIA LANIER

Introduction by
A. L. ROWSE

Clarkson N. Potter, Inc./Publishers

DISTRIBUTED BY CROWN PUBLISHERS, INC.

First published in the United States 1979
by Clarkson N. Potter, Inc./Publishers
One Park Avenue, New York, N.Y. 10016

Introduction © A. L. Rowse 1978

Published in Great Britain by
Jonathan Cape Ltd

Library of Congress Cataloging In Publication Data

Lanier, Emilia
The poems of Shakespeare's Dark Lady – Salve deus rex judaeorum.
1. Christian poetry, English.   2. Women – Poetry.
I. Rowse, Alfred Leslie, 1903 – II Title.
III. Title: Shakespeare's Dark Lady.
PR2296.L27S2 1979   821'.3   78–31141

ISBN 0–517–53745–1

Printed in Great Britain by Ebenezer Baylis and Son Limited
The Trinity Press, Worcester, and London

To
Sir John Gielgud
in recognition of his genius
as an interpreter of Shakespeare

Contents

Illustrations

Acknowledgments

Acknowledgment is due to the following for their kind permission to reproduce the illustrations: by gracious permission of Her Majesty the Queen ('Queen Elizabeth confounding the Goddesses'); the Fitzwilliam Musuem, Cambridge (Shakespeare's Southampton); the Greater London Council, Ranger's House (Katherine Knevet); the National Portrait Gallery (William Shakespeare, Queen Anne, Mary Sidney and Margaret Russell); the National Trust (Lady Arabella Stuart); the Lord Sackville, photograph by courtesy of the Courtauld Institute of Art (Anne Clifford); Somerset Archaeological and Natural History Society (Samuel Daniel); Statens Konstmuseer, Stockholm (Lucy Harington); L. G. Stopford Sackville (Lord Chamberlain Hunsdon); as in Roy Strong, *The English Icon* (Routledge, 1969), present whereabouts unknown (Susan Bertie).

Preface

I have entitled this volume *The Poems of Shakespeare's Dark Lady*, though in fact it contains her one long religious poem, with a number of dedicatory poems to James I's Queen, the Princess Elizabeth, Lady Arabella Stuart, and a number of other grand ladies, all of them countesses. The poem did not receive the attention the 'high-minded' authoress expected, and it has been entirely overlooked since, not even mentioned — except by Mr John Buxton, and he did not realise what he had in his hand.

In his admirable *Sir Philip Sidney and the English Renaissance* he refers to it as a 'work of somewhat long-winded piety' which mentions the unpublished translation which Sidney and his sister had made of the Psalms. (Actually Emilia Lanier was correct in claiming that his sister, Lady Pembroke's, versions of these were better than her brother's.) Mr Buxton continues: 'of "Mistress Æmilia Lanyer, wife to Captaine Alfonso Lanyer, Servant to the King's Majestie", as she describes herself, I know nothing. Her Christian name and her husband's, suggest that they may both have been Italian.' Her Christian name was, for she was the daughter of Baptista Bassano; her husband's was French. Both Bassanos and Laniers were intensely musical, prolific families of royal musicians at Court.

Nothing was known of Emilia Bassano, later Mistress Lanier, until Simon Forman told us who she was, in his voluminous and invaluable case-books in the Bodleian Library. She had been the mistress of Lord Chamberlain Hunsdon, the patron of Shakespeare's Company, until she was discarded and married off to the musician Lanier in October 1592. That gave me my clue. I need not recount here the exciting tracks I followed up, in which I was much helped by a number of fellow scholars; suffice it to say that every single detail consistently conformed and confirmed — character, circumstances, above all dating, which is determinative (and is especially an historian's province). If I had not been correct in my original findings about the *Sonnets*, and held to them against every discouragement from people who did not trouble even to follow the argument, I should never have discovered her.

Nobody knew anything about her; now we do know. In my Introduction I have brought together all the known facts about her, and written her biography. It is knowing her background that has given up her secret. This has revealed to us what a remarkable personality hers was in her own right. Everything corroborates Shakespeare's and Forman's rather shattering experience of her — though we must always remember what she experienced from the hands and tongues of men. This she greatly resented, as she resented (understandably) her ill chances in life. She provides the one case of an aggressive feminist that I know in the Elizabethan Age — and perhaps no wonder. Also she was the best woman poet in that age, except for Sidney's sister, the Countess of Pembroke — far better than the semi-divine Queen. This may be not saying much; all the same, it would be a mistake to underrate her competence as a poet. She had natural facility, and she was a highly educated woman; when one knows how little literate many great ladies of the time were, let alone women in general, one then realises how exceptional and superior (of this she was well aware) she was. I must now leave her to speak for herself.

Her book is of the utmost rarity: there are only four complete copies in the world. The Bodleian copy, which I have mostly worked with, is incomplete at the end; the British Library copy incomplete at the beginning. With the kind help of Dr Dennis Rhodes I have been able to supply each with a Xerox to fill in the missing section. I cannot sufficiently thank the Bodleian officials for their kindness to me over many years of research into Forman's papers, and for supplying me with Xeroxes of Emilia's work for comparative purposes. I am nostalgically grateful to the Huntington Library, where I researched for some happy years, for allowing me to compare their copy with others.

In the text I here print I have kept to the original spelling and lay-out, for what use it may be to fellow-workers in this field, since the original is so rare—rather against the principle my friend, Sir John Neale, and I agreed upon years ago to modernise Elizabethan spelling. However, Emilia's spelling is less rebarbative, rather more modern than usual, in fact; though one cannot tell how much that represents the printer. So what?—for once I make a concession in the matter.

In addition to the libraries where I have worked—especially the Bodleian at Oxford, where Forman's MSS are, a mine never worked until I came to them—I am much indebted for help to Dr John Guy of the Public Record Office, Mr Roger Prior, Miss Mary Edmond, Miss Joyce Batty and Lady Mander.

NEW YEAR   A.L.R.

1978

Shakespeare's Dark Lady

Shakespeare's *Sonnets* have been regarded, quite unnecessarily, as offering an insoluble problem. In fact, their problems have now been solved, with complete consistency, dating and all, and the answers cannot be questioned. If these answers were not correct, and the problems solved, they could easily be shown to be wrong. But they will not be, for they are the answer, obvious and definite — in a way, conservative for they are in keeping with all the known facts about Shakespeare, with tradition and common sense.

The trouble arose quite simply from the publisher, Thomas Thorpe, dedicating the Sonnets, in 1609, years after they were written, to a 'Mr W.H.' from whom he had got the manuscript. It cannot be sufficiently repeated that this Mr W.H. was Thorpe's dedicatee, not Shakespeare's young man in the Sonnets at all. Everyone knows that the T.T. who published the Sonnets was the publisher, Thomas Thorpe, who liked writing flowery dedications.

So — the young man in the Sonnets is *not* Thorpe's Mr W.H. All the books written on that misapprehension are complete rubbish. The young man of the Sonnets is the obvious person, Shakespeare's only patron, the Earl of Southampton, 'Lord of my love', to whom and for whom he wrote, and publicly dedicated his long narrative poems in 1593 and 1594. The Sonnets were written in this same period, 1592 to 1594–5; the years 1592 and 1593 were plague years, in which the theatres were largely closed, and Shakespeare had the time and leisure to write for his patron, on whom he was considerably dependent at this juncture, the turning point in his life.

In Elizabethan social usage it was quite regular to address a knight as Mr, i.e. Master — you could never address a lord as such. Sir Francis Bacon is sometimes referred to as Mr Bacon; Southampton's mother regularly referred to her second husband, Sir Thomas Heneage, as Mr Heneage. So Thorpe's dedicatee, Mr W.H., can be a knight, never a lord. Her third husband was a young man her son's age, Sir William Harvey.

Thorpe the publisher had reason to be grateful — so have we — to Mr W.H., the one and only person who had got the manuscript of the Sonnets for him (Shakespeare himself uses the word 'beget' simply for 'get'). In 1607 Southampton's mother died, leaving her household goods and chattels to Harvey. In 1608 he married a young woman, Cordelia Annesley; this is why next year, Thorpe wishes him 'all happiness and that eternity promised by our ever-living poet'. That is, quite simply the eternity the poet had promised Southampton years before, if only he would marry, produce children and carry on the family to posterity. It is really quite simple: 1607 — 1608 — 1609.

All this is fact. We are at liberty to conjecture, if we wish, where the manuscript came from — from the Countess's household goods. She, we know, had been anxious in those early 1590s to see her son do his duty by the family, marry and carry it on. The first section of the Sonnets is a persuasion to the ambivalent young man to do so — in vain. The young Lord did not involve himself in the toils of family life until very late in 1598, even then reluctantly — when his friend and leader, Essex, made him marry Elizabeth Vernon (Essex's cousin) in the last month of her pregnancy, only just in time. Thus the family was carried on, but that was more than three years after the period of the Sonnets, which ended in the winter of 1594–5.

It must be realised that Shakespeare did not publish his Sonnets any more than Sir Philip Sidney did his — much too autobiographical and near the bone. John Buxton tells us that Sidney's sonnets, *Astrophil and Stella*, circulated in two versions: 'one for Sidney's friends who knew Stella's identity and another for those who did not, and who could read the poems without discovering any secret passion by which Stella might be compromised.'[1] So with Shakespeare: we are told that

[1] John Buxton, *Sir Philip Sidney and the English Renaissance*, 184.

some of his 'sugared sonnets' circulated in manuscript—those would certainly not be the far from sugared ones about the Dark Lady, with their striking, tortured, defamatory portrait of her—like nothing else in Elizabethan literature. *All* the sonnets were written for the patron: Shakespeare was his poet, and the sonnets were in one aspect duty-sonnets, tribute from the poet to his patron. Shakespeare did not publish the Sonnets; they are badly proof-read, unlike *Venus and Adonis* and *The Rape of Lucrece*, which were printed by his Stratford acquaintance in Blackfriars and are carefully corrected. Thorpe was not Shakespeare's publisher: he was lucky to get such a snip and was correspondingly, confusingly, grateful.

Shakespeare did well to keep silence; the lady in question did not—as we can see from her violent reaction to the defaming portrait of her: the prose piece[1] she inserted in her book of poems entered for publication in 1610, the very year after the *Sonnets* had appeared, and actually published in 1611.

We do not need to recapitulate the fascinating story told in the Sonnets; though most people are unaware of it through not reading them in sequence, like a novel, but just picking one out here and there. In that way the story they tell is missed. Actually they fall into two groups. The first, Sonnets 1 to 126, describes the poet's relations with his young patron and friend, and they are in sequence as they are, running from 1592 to 1594–5, as an Elizabethan historian can corroborate from the topical references: the fall of Sir Walter Ralegh in 1592, the death of Marlowe in May 1593, the coinciding of Lopez's condemnation and execution with the surrender of Paris to Henri IV and the promise of peace in the early summer of 1594, to the rigorous campaign against Jesuits and seminarists in the winter of 1594–5. Perfectly straightforward and intelligible to an Elizabethan historian who knows the events of those years from month to month. Anyone who does not cannot be expected to get it right — hence the intolerable confusion with which the subject has been surrounded, now at last cleared up.

[1] See pp. 77–8.

The second section of the Sonnets, 127 to 152, centres upon Shakespeare's tormented relations with the Lady, and in time they fall within the first sequence. That is to say, the affair with her fell in 1592 and 1593. This is corroborated by *Love's Labour's Lost* of 1593, a skit on the Southampton circle by its poet, in which it is well known that the Dark Lady appears as Rosaline and Shakespeare himself as Berowne. There appears the happier, gayer side of his relations with the lady. In the *Rape of Lucrece*, of later 1593 (published in 1594) we move into the darker, guilt-tormented atmosphere into which the relationship moved before it was broken off.

The basic fact of the whole story is the poet's relationship with his patron. The actor-playwright would not have been received in this cultivated, aristocratic circle if it had not been for this. More, he might not have survived the strain of those plague years, as he tells us, if it had not been for the young Lord's support. Robert Greene and Thomas Watson died in 1592; Marlowe was killed in 1593; Kyd disappeared in the next twelvemonth, Peele not long after.

A great deal is known about young Southampton as a promising star at Court, an earl, ward of Lord Treasurer Burghley, noble connections on every side. He was well educated (at St John's, Cambridge, to which he left a collection of books), cultivated, ambitious to shine in action, on land or at sea, as also in the arts — he was much dedicated to and painted. He was, like his family, Catholic but not a *dévot* and certainly not a political Catholic; under James I he conformed and ultimately advocated and led a forward Protestant policy. Essex had great influence with him in this direction; Southampton looked up to him as leader and friend. The relationship, which was warm and affectionate, was also hot-headed and led on to disaster. (Something of this was glanced at by Shakespeare in the Achilles-Patroclus relationship in *Troilus and Cressida*.)

But this is going beyond the bounds of our subject, though it is true that Southampton was a delayed adolescent and, I am bound to confess that — like some other Elizabethan aristocrats — he was wilful and spoiled. On the other hand, his nature was golden and good, loyal and generous to a fault. In 1592 to 1594 we have to deal with one who was not much more than a youth: born on 6th October, 1573 he was only nineteen to twenty-one in those years. He had been orphaned, left without a father at the age of six—and this accounted for something in his make-up. His mother was, from all the evidence, a charming woman who had been badly treated by her foolish husband. The boy became an earl on his father's death. Rather feminine in appearance, with his long lock over one shoulder, he was during the period of the Sonnets, ambivalent, not yet sexually directed. Everything shows that William Shakespeare was strongly heterosexual, deeply responsive to women. The Sonnets make it perfectly clear that he is not interested in the youth sexually; his love for him—and he had every reason to love this generous benefactor, this golden youth—was what is called platonic. There was plenty of that in the Renaissance—compare Fulke Greville's love for Philip Sidney. (Marlowe and Francis Bacon, however, were outright homosexuals.)

There is an element of the tutorial in Shakespeare's attitude, almost as if he spoke *in loco parentis*. After all, he was nearly ten years older, and the youth had no father; he disliked his guardian, the great Lord Burghley. (All the young nobles who were his wards turned against this prosy old Polonius, for all his virtues: Southampton, Bedford, Rutland all sided with Essex.) Generous and cultivated as he was, Southampton was much made up to by other writers. The young Nashe tried to bounce himself into his favour with an unsolicited dedication; for a brief period before Marlowe's death he was received favourably by the Earl, and was writing *Hero and Leander* in competition with *Venus and Adonis* when he was killed. This is the Rival Poet of the Sonnets. There are several indications that Marlowe and Shakespeare, such very different characters, were better known to each other than has been realised.

Before the brief rivalry with Marlowe for Southampton's favour, something had occurred to tarnish the golden youth's innocence, a complication for which Shakespeare—he was indeed honest[1] and of an

[1] In Elizabethan English 'honest' means 'honourable', as does the Latin *honestus*.

[5]

open and free nature, Ben Jonson witnessed — reproached himself. It was from this that the dubious and questionable, the agonising (for Shakespeare) triangular relationship sprang, the story unfolded. Shakespeare regarded himself as responsible, as he was. In regular Elizabethan fashion he got a social superior, his patron, to write to the Lady he desired access to. The Lady, being what she was, took the opportunity to inveigle the young Earl into her clutches. She was a woman of ill repute; her bad reputation besmirched them both, since she was well known. More, this appears to have been the golden youth's initiation into sex relations with a woman — when he wouldn't marry properly and do his duty for the family. Shakespeare is especially grieved, for he feels responsible and fears for the young Lord's reputation, his character and his health.

Who was this woman who was quite well known at the time, though obliterated by the lapse of nearly four hundred years?

⤞ II ⤝

We must concentrate, first, on what Shakespeare tells us about her: he tells us a great deal, though he very properly withholds her name, as Sidney had done Stella's (i.e. Penelope, Lady Rich, Essex's sister).

The first thing Shakespeare tells us is that she is very dark: raven black eyes, eyelashes, eyebrows — 'her eyes so suited' — and black hair. This was unfashionable in the Elizabethan age, when a fair complexion and Venetian red hair were the fashion. There were people who said that her looks were not such as to compel love — so she was quite well known to them at least. The next thing we are told is that she was musical, and had the accomplishment of playing on the virginals. The third thing is that her deeds were black, for she was engaged in torturing Shakespeare by trying to inveigle his young patron, wounding their friendship, creating suspicion and anxiety for Shakespeare.

Next, that she had taken the opportunity of Southampton's writing to her on his poet's behalf to get hold of the young man. We learn that she is promiscuous, and being disingenuous with him; yet Shakespeare cannot help himself, he is completely subjugated. His position is a humiliating one, reduced as he is to ask for a share in her love, enjoyed by others. Shakespeare next confesses himself uncertain and tortured by anxiety as to her relations with the golden youth:

> The better angel is a man right fair,
> The worser spirit a woman coloured ill.

He supposes 'one angel in another's hell': this means what those who know Elizabethan bawdy (and even modern slang) will recognise. And when he says that he lives in doubt 'till my bad angel fire my good one out', this carries the Elizabethan connotation, familiar enough in contemporary drama, especially Shakespeare's, or in medical evidence, as with Clowes or Forman, of the ever-present danger of venereal disease at the time.

From this point Shakespeare confesses that his love is as a fever, making him 'frantic-mad with unrest'; it is contrary to reason and the evidence of his own eyes which recognise her falseness to him. While 'the world' knows her for what she is, his infatuation blinds him from recognising what he knows to be the truth. He himself takes her side against those who hate her. But whence has she 'this powerful might ... to make me give the lie to my true sight'? He is more infatuated even when he sees 'just cause of hate' and 'what others do abhor' in her. So, again, she is a person well known in their circle. Shakespeare is in a humiliating situation when he is reduced to plead that she should not 'abhor my state ... with others', i.e. join others in looking down on him. His very love for her sprang out of pity for her situation:

> If thy unworthiness raised love in me,
> More worthy I to be beloved of thee.

With that openness of nature Jonson pointed to, so that Shakespeare was not the man to mystify anyone, or to shrink from confessing his own sin, he admits candidly that he has broken his word or vow, and is 'forsworn'; but she is twice 'forsworn' in swearing love to him, 'in

[7]

act thy bed-vow broke and new faith torn'. This suggests that she, like him, was already married, but that she had also broken her word that she would continue his love to him. They were thus both alike perjured.

At this point the relationship breaks off—with Shakespeare,

> I, sick withal, the help of bath desired,
> And thither hied, a sad distempered guest.

The word 'thither' indicates a place; the relationship broken off, he would appear to have gone to Bath, where Elizabethans regularly went for treatment for venereal infection. The second Lord Chamberlain Hunsdon resorted to Bath for the same reason; so, too, Robert Cecil, Lord Salisbury, according to his former friend Ralegh. Nothing improbable in that: venereal disease was rife in Elizabethan London.

We glean more information by turning back to the Southampton Sonnets, which view the triangular complication from the point of view of the two men and their relationship. With his charming candour Shakespeare takes the blame upon himself, 'myself corrupting ... Excusing thy sins' and the youth's 'sensual fault'. Shakespeare is afraid that his own guilt 'should do thee shame' and injure Southampton's reputation:

> Nor thou with public kindness honour me,
> Unless thou take that honour from thy name.

Once more, we see that the affair is known in their circle, and so are all three involved.

Once more it is brought home that Shakespeare's situation between these two is a humiliating one; he even ventures on a reproach:

> I do forgive thy robbery, gentle thief,
> Although thou steal thee all my poverty.

The reproach is made quite directly:

> Ay me! but yet thou mightst my seat forbear ...

[8]

The loss of his 'good angel', his friend and patron, to whom he owes so much, touches him more deeply. All the same, it is painful to have to say:

> Take all my loves, my love, yea, take them all.

Though this may stand for Shakespeare's generosity of mind, of an older to a younger, nevertheless the poet had little option, considering that this was his young patron on whom, until the foundation of the Lord Chamberlain's Company next year, 1594, he was dependent.

We may reflect that there was much less danger of Southampton, with his ambivalent nature, coming under the thumb, the potent spell, which Shakespeare underwent:

> O, from what power hast thou this powerful might ...
> There is such strength and warrantise of skill ...
> The more I hear and see just cause of hate?

We must remember, also, that this was the man's account of the relationship; we do not have the woman's side to it. We must in justice remember that, as no one has had the imagination to do. This was the portrait of herself with which the Lady was confronted when Thomas Thorpe got the manuscript of the Sonnets years later and published them in 1609. No wonder Shakespeare was not responsible; he did well to keep silence.

➣ III ➢

We must turn to the Lady herself, and her side of the matter.

Here the information of Simon Forman is of crucial importance.[1] 'Dr' Forman had long been known to Shakespeare scholars for his firsthand accounts of having seen several of Shakespeare's plays— *The Winter's Tale, Macbeth, Cymbeline, Richard II*—at the Globe in April 1611. Authentically in keeping with his own interests—he

---

[1] For references in detail v. my *The Case-Books of Simon Forman* (paperback edition).

combined astrology with medicine, in the Elizabethan manner—he was mainly taken by the witches in Macbeth, Autolycus the pedlar-thief, by coincidences and foretellings, cozening and cheating. But no one had penetrated Forman's papers in depth for the extraordinary amount of reliable information they give about hundreds of Eliza-bethans of all classes of society from the highest to the lowest. They range from the two Frances Howards—one to become Duchess of Richmond and Lennox, the other, daughter of the Earl and Countess of Suffolk, to become Countess of Somerset and poisoner of Sir Thomas Overbury—down through the wife of a dean and mistresses of various clerics to humble sailors' wives and tarts. Two clients were daughters of the first Lord Hunsdon, Lord Chamberlain, patron of the Lord Chamberlain's Company (Shakespeare's company); Lady Hoby and Lady Scrope (a lady-in-waiting to the Queen), her first cousins once removed. Hunsdon's son, the second Lord Chamberlain Hunsdon, had long known Forman from early days, when Forman had visited him as governor of the Isle of Wight.

The first Hunsdon owned a house in Blackfriars and occasionally stayed there: the second Hunsdon had his town house there. Shake-speare's Stratford acquaintance, Richard Field, who printed *Venus and Adonis* and the *Rape of Lucrece*, had his printing press in Blackfriars. The theatre manager, James Burbage, had started as the first Lord Chamberlain Hunsdon's man. He was the active agent in forming the Lord Chamberlain's Company with Shakespeare as a partner; later he bought the Blackfriars theatre, with Shakespeare as a part owner. *The Tempest* was based on a manuscript narrative of the tornado and wreck on Bermuda by William Strachey, who brought it back to Blackfriars in 1611. This small circle, connected with the theatre and with Shakespeare, pivoted upon Blackfriars. One cannot overestimate the importance of this, hitherto little realised.

On 17th May, 1597—that is, a couple of years after Shakespeare's Sonnets for Southampton came to an end, with the winter of 1594–5— Emilia Lanier came to consult Forman. Forman, after his regular manner, collects what information he can about his client; it was necessary that it should be as accurate as possible for the casting of a horoscope. What is extraordinary about Forman is the accuracy of his information on the whole, when checked against external evidence — quite remarkable when one considers people's endemic inaccuracy, particularly when the information comes verbally. But, of course, Forman was trained in this, had a powerful memory — and Elizabethans trained and relied on memory much more than we do.

Forman tells us that Mrs Lanier was born a Bassano — actually she was the daughter of one of the Queen's Italian musicians, Baptista Bassano, and his 'reputed wife', Margaret Johnson: so she was illegitimate to begin with. He wrote down: 'she hath had hard fortune in her youth. Her father died when she was young; the wealth of her father failed before he died, and he began to be miserable in his estate.' We are brought up short by what we next learn: 'she was paramour to my old Lord Hunsdon that was Lord Chamberlain, and was maintained in great pride; being with child she was for colour married to a minstrel', i.e. Alphonso Lanier, another of the Queen's musicians.

On her next visit, 3rd June, we learn that she had been brought up with the Countess of Kent and had been married four years, but the old Lord Chamberlain had kept her long. 'She was maintained in great pomp. She is high-minded — she hath something in her mind she would have done for her. She hath £40 a year and was wealthy to him that married her, in money and jewels. She can hardly keep secret. She was very brave in youth. She hath many false conceptions. She hath a son, his name is Henry' — after his father, the Lord Chamberlain. This son also became in time one of the royal musicians.

On 16th June she comes to inquire whether her husband shall come to any preferment before he comes home again. He had gone to serve, hoping for preferment, in the Islands Voyage of this year, in which Southampton figured as commander of the *Garland*. Lanier served as a gentleman volunteer. Next we learn what she really wanted, whether she shall be a lady, i.e. of title — so many knights were made on these expeditions. How should she speed? She told Forman that she hath been favoured much of her Majesty and of many noble men, hath had great gifts and been made much of — a nobleman that is dead hath loved her well and kept her. But her husband hath dealt hardly with her, hath spent and consumed her goods. She is now very needy, in debt and it seems for lucre's sake will be a good fellow, for necessity doth compel. She hath a wart or mole in the pit of the throat or near it.

Forman appended a note to the effect that the husband was at sea on Essex's Islands Voyage 'in hope to be knighted, though there was little cause why he should'. His wife demanded to know 'whether she should be a lady or no'. Forman added later : 'he was not knighted nor yet worthy thereof', nor was she worthy to be a lady. But he was not the one to neglect the opportunity of the husband's absence and the wife's readiness 'for lucre's sake to be a good fellow'.

He put the question for himself: 'a certain man longed to see a gentlewoman whom he loved and desired to halek with.' ('Halek' is his regular code-word for 'to have sex with'.) He sent his man to inquire, by whom 'she sent word that if his master came he shall be welcome. He went and supped with her and stayed all night. She was familiar and friendly to him in all things, but only she would not halek. Yet he felt all parts of her body willingly and kissed her often, but she would not do in any wise. Whereupon he took some displeasure.' To this he added a note, 'but yet they were friends again afterwards'; and another note, 'she was a whore and dealt evil with him after'.

Twelve days later, after failing to comply with an invitation to come to her, 'next afternoon she sent her maid to me and I went with her to her'. A month later he put the question 'whether to go to Lanier's this night or no'; she sent both her man and maid to fetch him : 'I went with them and stayed all night.' At the end of the year he is questioning what happens concerning her tales as to the invocation of spirits, whether or not she is an incuba, 'and whether I shall end it or no'. These equivocal contacts continued for some time, for on 7th January, 1600 Forman casts 'to know why Mrs Lanier sent for me, what will follow, and whether she intendeth any more villainy'. In the extensive menagerie of Forman's womenfolk she is the only one who seems to have given him cause for alarm. Evidently a powerful personality, commanding him to come to her, allowing him every liberty except the last on their first night; first she wouldn't, then she would — distracting and disturbing Forman, as Shakespeare's dark and musical woman drove him 'frantic-mad' by her temperamental treatment of him. Shakespeare's word for her was 'tyrannous', Forman's 'high-minded'; Shakespeare said that she looked down on him and demeaned him in talk with others, abhorring his state — Forman that she couldn't keep secret, she talked. We need not hold it against her that she was snobbish; most humans, and all Elizabethans, are class-conscious and want to move up in the social scale. Shakespeare tells us that she was a woman of ill repute, and people did not think her beautiful; Forman calls her angrily 'a whore', and wondered whether she was an incuba dealing with the spirits — not an unfamiliar notion to an Elizabethan.

O, from what power hast thou this powerful might?

We must not, however, make the mistake of an Eng. Lit. scholar at Oxford and dismiss her with — 'but there were hundreds of whores in Elizabethan London.' Most imperceptive — for this woman was a very special case: the recognised mistress of the Lord Chamberlain himself, who was the Queen's first cousin and, moreover, patron of Shakespeare's company. How much closer could one expect to get?

What Forman tells us is corroborated by external evidence. Emilia, daughter of Baptista Bassano, had been christened at St Botolph, Bishopsgate, on 27th January, 1569 — which would make her over twenty-eight when she first consulted Forman, though she told him twenty-four. She was then living in Longditch, Westminster, next to Canon Row, a fashionable quarter full of the houses of grandees, like Sir Edward Hoby, and the Earls of Hertford, Derby and Lincoln.[1] Bishopsgate and Shoreditch were where the foreign musicians and

---

[1] John Stow, *A Survey of London*, ed. C. L. Kingsford, ii. 102, 374–5.

theatre-folk lived—Shakespeare himself, as we know, in the 1590s. The Bassanos were a numerous clan who came into this country from Venice in the later years of Henry VIII, when Italian artists as well as musicians were propagating Renaissance influences. The Laniers were French, from Rouen, who came in a generation later with Elizabeth I.[1]

In 1563 we learn, from a Star Chamber reference, that there had been 'a conspiracy to murder' Baptista Bassano, for which Henry Dingley was condemned to be whipped and pilloried and to perpetual imprisonment in Bridewell, and Mark Antony to be banished out of the realm.[2] Bassano was buried in Bishopsgate on 11th May, 1576, leaving two orphan girls, Emilia at seven, and Angela who later married Joseph Holland. Their mother Margaret Johnson was buried there on 7th July, 1587, leaving Emilia to take the chances of life. She had been left a dowry of £100, though we may doubt if she ever received it: she told Forman that she had been brought up by the Countess of Kent—presumably as a girl waiting on her, with her Italian looks and musical talent, it is not too much to assume.

About this time she would have been taken up and kept as his mistress by Lord Chamberlain Hunsdon. He was the son of Henry VIII's discarded mistress by Mary Boleyn, Anne Boleyn's sister, by William Carey to whom she had been married off. A soldierly type, he was much of his time on the Scottish Border as Lord Warden of the East Marches and governor of Berwick, where, in addition to a large family, he had an illegitimate son who became a (perhaps understandably) celibate bishop of Exeter. Sir Robert Naunton gives us a clear picture of him.

He was a fast man to his Prince, and firm to his friends and servants; and though he might speak big and therein would be borne out, yet was he not the more dreadful but less harmful, and far from the

---

[1] Not Italian, as Mr Buxton says, *op. cit.*, 236.
[2] I owe this reference, from the lost registers of Star Chamber, to the kindness of Dr John Guy of the P.R.O. The Extracts from these are now at the Huntington Library, Ellesmere MS. 2652, fo. 13.

practice of my Lord of Leicester's instructions, for he was down-right. [Leicester was always smooth and disingenuous.] I have heard those that knew him well say merrily of him that his Latin and his dissimulation were both alike; and that his custom of swearing and obscenity in speaking made him seem a worse Christian than he was, and a better Knight of the Carpet than he should be. As he lived in a ruffling time, so he loved sword and buckler men, and such as our fathers were wont to call men of their hands ... And this is one that stood amongst the *Togati*, of an honest stout heart, and such a one as upon occasion would have fought for his Prince and his country; for he had the charge of the Queen's person, both in the Court and the Camp at Tilbury.[1]

That was when the Armada was upon the coast in 1588. In short, a rough, manly soldier, but he had an ear for music — several compositions were dedicated to him — and an eye (not only an eye) for a nubile girl.

When Emilia proved pregnant, she was discarded (as Hunsdon's mother had been) with a good *dot* and married off on 18th October, 1592 to Alphonso Lanier, also at St Botolph, Bishopsgate.[2] Her son by the Lord Chamberlain was named Henry after him: she had a daughter, presumably by her husband, Odilla — a rather stuck-up name — who lived only nine months and was also buried at St Botolph's. Her telling Forman that she had been married four years was quite correct, and she added that she was miserable and unhappy with Lanier. No doubt it was a comedown from the pomp and pride of being the Lord Chamberlain's *maîtresse en titre*. What is significant is that this, 1592–3, is precisely the time when the charming actor-dramatist fell in love with her out of compassion for her condition and unhappy state:

> If thy unworthiness raised love in me,
> More worthy I to be beloved of thee.

[1] Sir Robert Naunton, *Fragmenta Regalia* (Arber's English Reprints), 46–7.
[2] I am indebted to Miss Mary Edmond for these entries from the registers of St Botolph's, Bishopsgate.

We may, in conclusion, say that it is not surprising that Shakespeare's Dark Lady should turn up among Forman's clients, for so also did Shakespeare's known landlady, the French Madame Montjoie (or Mountjoy), of Silver Street, just around the corner from Bishopsgate. It is just that no one had bothered to search Forman's voluminous casebooks in the Bodleian, waiting there all the time to be searched in depth, just where she would turn up, if anywhere.

When we enter the realm of imaginative creations, as opposed to the autobiographical such as the Sonnets, we are dealing with the conjectural. We need both intellectual perception and intuitive subtlety; for, while we realise that a real writer's experience enters into his creations, we must be careful not to make too crude identifications between the creations and persons within his experience. Everyone knows that, throughout the whole of literature, there are such identifications: that Squire Allworthy in Fielding's *Tom Jones* was Ralph Allen, for example, or Harold Skimpole in *Bleak House* was based on Leigh Hunt.

When Shakespeare came to write *Antony and Cleopatra* in 1606 did he have anyone in mind in his portrait of Cleopatra? Everyone has noticed that her strongly etched character is unparalleled in his work. She is an extraordinarily strong personality, mercurial and changing, temperamental and tempestuous, but bewitching. She laid a spell on Antony. She was an alien, a dark gipsy; an unpopular personality, she was strong-willed, highly intelligent but undependable: in the end, she let Antony down and deserted him at Actium.

Even Dover-Wilson felt impelled to say, à propos of *Antony and Cleopatra* (and Agatha Christie agreed with him):

many believe that Plutarch's tale of a fickle swarthy mistress, and an infatuated lover who finds it impossible to fling free, had a personal interest for the poet who was confessing, somewhere about 1594 apparently, that a woman 'as black as hell, as dark as night' left him 'past cure

And frantic-mad with evermore unrest'.

If so the emotion was now remembered in tranquillity, for he had freed himself from his former enchantment, as he had from the strain of sex-nausea which seems to run through the tragedies up to and including *King Lear*.

The cautious historian will only go so far as to note, what others have noted, that, over the passionate infatuation of Antony and Cleopatra, there plays an enigmatic smile. Certainly, whatever experience was behind it, Shakespeare had flung free. A writer writes out of his troubles of mind and heart, and also writes himself out of them.

❧ IV ❧

We must now turn to what Emilia tells us of herself in the long religious poem she published in 1611, *Salve Deus Rex Judæorum* (Hail, God, King of the Jews)—a title which she dreamed, she tells us, years before she ever thought of writing her poem. Perhaps it came to her at the time of her conversion—for, since the time we last heard of her from Forman, she has undergone a religious conversion. With her powerful temperament this is not surprising: she had plenty to be converted from—and, as might be expected, she throws herself passionately into her religious stance; with unmitigated advocacy, she goes the whole hog.

What is more surprising is that she is a fair poet, far superior to the Queen, for example, who wrote antiquated doggerel. In fact, except for Sidney's sister, the Countess of Pembroke, Emilia is the best woman poet of the age. This is not saying much, but it is to be observed that she has an easy natural command of iambic pentameter— all her verses are in that measure—and she has no less easy a command of rhymes. Her defect indeed is that she was too facile and fluent: she wrote too much, she padded out what she had to say—it would have been more effective if shorter. (One remembers what Forman said about her talking too much, she can 'hardly keep secret'.)

On the other hand, she reveals herself a highly educated woman, well read in the Bible and the classics patronised by the Renaissance.

She has a gift for words—quite exceptional to anyone acquainted with the comparative illiteracy of even famous Elizabethan women, Lady Ralegh, Bess of Hardwick, Mary Fitton, or others of the Queen's ladies-in-waiting. Very few women in the age—only notoriously well educated ones like Mary Sidney or the Cooke sisters—could rival her. She has complete power of expression, if verbose and redundant; occasionally she uses rare words, or has an apt and memorable turn of phrase, even a moving line, for all her rhetorical exaggeration in keeping with her temperament.

In versification she is close to Samuel Daniel, and this is natural, for he belonged to the circle of which she became a member. Margaret, Countess of Cumberland was a patroness, with her daughter, Lady Anne Clifford, Countess of Dorset and subsequently of Pembroke and Montgomery. Daniel was tutor to the daughter. Let us remember, also, that Daniel was brother-in-law to the Italian, part-Jewish, John Florio, who was tutor to Southampton and for some years lived in his household. Shakespeare was well acquainted with Florio and, in the early 1590s, Shakespeare's Sonnets were closest to Daniel's. There were interchanges between Shakespeare and Daniel, Shakespeare drawing on Daniel's *Civil Wars* for *Richard II*, Daniel revising his *Tragedy of Cleopatra* in the light of *Antony and Cleopatra*.

On the title-page Emilia describes herself as 'Mistris Æmilia [characteristically upstage] Lanyer, Wife to Captain Alfonso Lanyer, Servant to the Kings Majestie'. He had been one of the fifty-nine musicians who played at Queen Elizabeth's funeral and was now one of King James I's musicians. She was tied to him in spite of the derogatory report of him she had given Forman. Nor can we rely on what she said of him being gospel-truth any more than accept her age as being that which she told Forman—four years younger than she really was. For, in the interval between that and the publication of her book, we have a testimonial of good character for Alfonso Lanier from an impeccable source, good Bishop Bancroft of London, shortly to become Archbishop of Canterbury. On 24th August, 1604 Bancroft wrote to Robert Cecil, then Lord Cranborne:

William Shakespeare

Henry Carey
Lord Hunsdon

ÆTATIS SVÆ 60
AN: 1591.

Lord Chamberlain Hunsdon

Captain Alfonso Lanier, the late Queen's and now his Majesty's servant, mine old fellow and loving friend, has obtained a suit of his Highness for the weighing of hay and straw about London. He was put in hope of your favour by the Earl of Southampton ... I therefore very heartily entreat you on his behalf. He did her Majesty good service in Ireland and in some other employments, whereby he has decayed his estate; and we served both together the Lord Chancellor, which makes me the bolder to crave your acceptance of my desire of good success to his said bill.

Whether as the result of this weighty advocacy or no, Cecil implemented Lanier's grant of this little monopoly. Let us observe that Alfonso would not have been 'mine old fellow and loving friend' to Bishop Bancroft if he had been a bad man: Emilia had denigrated him as she had done Shakespeare and frightened Forman. Southampton had intervened on Lanier's behalf. The mention of Ireland and 'some other employments' indicates the services upon which Southampton and Lanier had been employed at the same time, and we now learn that they knew each other. Is it likely, since Southampton knew the husband, that he did not know the wife? *Love's Labour's Lost* had been written in 1593, at the time of the Sonnets, as a skit on the Southampton circle by its poet-dramatist — on the theme with which the Sonnets begin, but do not continue, the young Lord's reluctance to engage with women. In it the actor-poet portrayed himself as Berowne, and his Dark Lady as Rosaline, for the amusement of his patron.

We know that Archbishop Bancroft, who did his best to restrain the intolerable Puritans, was devoted to music: he bequeathed all his musical instruments to his nephew.[1] He had been in the service of Lord Chancellor Ellesmere, probably as his chaplain, Alfonso in some other capacity. Alfonso's grant must have been a profitable one: 6d on every hayload, 3d on every load of straw, brought to London and Westminster, to run for twenty years. When he died in 1613 Emilia made

[1] Cf. my *The Elizabethan Renaissance: The Cultural Achievement*, 319.

it over to his brother Innocent, who later passed it to Clement Lanier, and thereby ensued a peck of troubles, recriminations, law-suits for years—she was a troublesome customer, aggressively pressing her rights.

Her book was printed by Valentine Simmes—who had printed several of Shakespeare's plays—for Richard Bonian, to be sold at his shop in St Paul's churchyard. The most remarkable thing about this little volume is the prose address 'To the Vertuous Reader', which is inserted between the main long poem and the many dedicatory poems which Emilia offers to grandees—James's Queen, Princess Elizabeth, the Lady Arabella Stuart, and the various Countesses of Kent, Pembroke, Cumberland, Suffolk, Bedford, Dorset. For all her conversion she had not ceased to be 'high-minded', noticeably upstage; and so strong is her personality, her egoism and sense of self that it comes through in every line she writes and makes it easy to read her character.

Her prose address is a piece of rampant feminism, like nothing else in the age—though a strong assertion of feminism runs all through the poems too, culminating in a passionate defence of Eve and putting the blame for eating the fatal apple on Adam! It is obvious that something personal had aroused her anger. Shakespeare's Sonnets had been published, though not by him, in 1609, with their unforgettable portrait of the woman who had driven him 'frantic-mad', dark and musical, tyrannical and temperamental, promiscuous and false, a powerful and overbearing personality, quite well known, of bad reputation. (Perhaps those Sonnets were intended as a warning to the young patron for whom they were written: he certainly did not fall under her spell as his susceptible poet had done—though she told Forman that she had been 'favoured ... of many noblemen' and received great gifts. This was exaggeration typical of her, and of her poems). The portrait was defamatory enough. The very next year, 1610, her book was announced, and in 1611 published.

In her angry prose riposte she reproved women for speaking ill of their own sex and spreading scandal about them. All women do not deserve to be blamed, and they should leave this to 'evil disposed men who—forgetting they were born of women, nourished by women, and that, if it were not by the means of women, they would be quite extinguished out of the world and a final end of them all—do like Vipers deface the wombs wherein they were bred.' Emilia was certainly a good hater, *à l'italienne*. Women were to take no notice of the imputations laid upon them by men other than to use them to their own benefit, as spurs to virtue. She then cites the wise and virtuous women from the Old Testament who had brought down the pride and arrogance of men. Cruel Sisera had been done in by Jael; wicked Haman overthrown by beautiful Esther, Holofernes by the courage of Judith, the unjust Elders by chaste Susanna.

Moreover, it had pleased Jesus Christ to be begotten of a woman, born of a woman, nourished by and obedient to a woman; he healed pardoned and comforted women. In his last agony he took care to make disposition of a woman; after his resurrection he appeared first to a woman. We notice, however, the tell-tale fact that, in all her long poem, there is no mention of Mary Magdalen, the repentant prostitute. The emphasis is all on virtue and chastity—wearisomely so; it is in character for her to go on and on about it, to be emphatic and to exaggerate. Virtuous women have been confessors and martyrs in all ages; it therefore becomes honourably minded men 'to speak reverently of our sex' and cherish virtue where they find it, putting the best interpretation upon it rather than give it 'wrong constructions'.

We see that Emilia has been personally piqued by something, as also that she is supercilious about others, ready to be censorious and to lay down the law.

We are not concerned with the religious or even the poetic aspect of her poems, we are concerned with the personal; we are looking for information about her. Fortunately, she is such an egoist that there is plenty of it—she herself stands in the forefront of almost every line—but we could wish for more information about other people. The dedicatory poems do at any rate give us some information about the great ladies she knew, and some she didn't know.

From her first page — a poem dedicated to James I's Queen — Emilia calls attention to that rarity, 'a woman's writing of divinest things'. Her reference to the Three Goddesses — Juno, Pallas and Venus — striving for the golden apple from Paris, reminds us of the famous portrait of Elizabeth I in that scene. Had Emilia seen that picture at Court? She repeats here what she had told Forman, that she had been favoured by Queen Elizabeth in her youth, and that Susan, Countess of Kent, was 'the mistress of my youth', 'guide of my ungoverned days'. The Countess herself had been directed by her famous mother, the highly Protestant Catherine Bertie, Duchess of Suffolk, who in Queen Mary's reign had peregrinated abroad for religion. 'No future profit is expected' from Susan, now the dowager Countess — which was just as well, for she was pretty hard up. Emilia herself lives shut up 'in sorrow's cell' — though we note that her husband is still alive. She has long been known by the Lady Arabella, though not so well as she wished. No doubt.

A longish poem, 'The Author's Dream', is dedicated to the dowager Countess of Pembroke. In it we notice that 'chariot' was pronounced 'charret', 'cuirasse' 'currat', and we encounter unexpectedly the infrequent word 'umpire'. Emilia knows of the Psalms written 'newly' by the Countess, though unpublished, and she prefers them to her brother's, Philip Sidney's — as she preferred Eve to Adam: why should Eve be 'defamed by more faulty men'? The next dedication is to the celebrated Lucy Harington, Countess of Bedford, patroness and friend of Donne: an intellectual woman, she is saluted for her knowledge and 'clear judgment'. There follows a rhetorical, sycophantic dedication to Margaret, Countess dowager of Cumberland: so this was written after 1605, when her privateering, tilting, sporting husband had died. This was the religious Margaret Russell, a Protestant who had found herself a fish out of water in the Catholic society of Cumberland: she is one of the 'elected souls' of whom Emilia now regarded herself as one.

The following dedication to Katherine, Countess of Suffolk, reads ironically after what was shortly to happen to her and her family — a fate apt to attend sycophantic flattery. Emilia regrets that she is a 'stranger' to her,

> Whose beauty, wisdom, children, high estate,
> Do all concur to make you fortunate.

The Countess was happy in her 'most honourable Lord', who had won fame at sea as Lord Thomas Howard—though we remember that he had retreated before the Spanish fleet in the Azores, perhaps wisely, leaving Sir Richard Grenville to his fate. This noble couple enjoyed the blessings of wealth—they were currently building Audley End, three times the size of the palace that is left. James I said that it was too grand for a king, but very well for a Lord Treasurer. (It was built out of embezzling funds from the Treasury.) Emilia awards them the blessings of honour and noble daughters. One of these was a client of Forman's, the Countess of Somerset who poisoned Sir Thomas Overbury in the Tower. We are assured of the Countess's 'pure, bright, and holy fires': it suffices to say that she was grasping and avaricious, drove her husband on to embezzle from the Treasury and take a pension from Spain, and was said to be the mistress of Robert Cecil.

The poem to Lady Anne Clifford, at this time Countess of Dorset, is interesting for the oblique light it throws on Emilia herself in what she says about birth. We are told that 'titles of honour which the world bestows' belong properly only to the virtuous. We, however, recall the pertinacity with which she pursued Forman to know whether her husband would acquire one. (He never did—he would have done from James I, had he money enough.) What difference was there when the world began, when all sprang from one woman and one man:

> Then how doth Gentry come to rise and fall?
> Or who is he that very rightly can
> Distinguish of his birth, or tell at all
> In what mean state his ancestors have been,
> Before some one of worth did honour win?

Emilia might well, with her own illegitimacy, argue that, and we may regard much of her moralising as but sour grapes. As to the successors to him who has won a title, although they bear his name,

> How do we know they spring out of the same
> True stock of honour, being not of that kind?

How do we know, we may well ask.

Only virtue deserves honour, we are told; if Emilia had been a man we might call her a poacher turned gamekeeper. As it is, we recognise the familiar psychological phenomenon of silly humans, of turning over a new leaf, becoming chaste and virtuous, when they have ceased to be young and attractive and nobody wants them. Lady Anne Clifford had had the seeds of virtue sown in her by her pious mother (this was as well, for her husband, the Earl of Dorset, was a riotous spendthrift and waster who treated her badly). Her birth and the careful education she received, combined with her godly heart, were better than worldly wealth (really? the disappointed console themselves by despising what they have missed).

> This world is but a stage where all do play their parts ...
> Here's no respect of persons, youth, nor age.

Lady Anne's mother, the dowager Countess of Cumberland, was Emilia's patroness, who had commanded her to write 'praiseful lines of that delightful place — Cookham', whither she had evidently accompanied the two ladies in *villeggiatura*. Emilia's own 'sad soul' was well able to sympathise with the 'inward cares', the 'afflictions' and 'trials' of the Countess. There had been a breach between her and the Earl in his last years; and he had left the Clifford estates away from his daughter, to his brother who inherited the earldom. There followed years of quarrels and litigation; mother and daughter felt that they had been cheated of their right. Emilia's temper flares up as she thinks of wicked worldlings enjoying the distress of the poor (she had been worldly and high-minded herself, and hated being poor). Now let the Lord rain down fire and brimstone on the mighty and raise up the poor and those in distress — like herself. Here is the same old temper, vindictive and revengeful, for all her conversion.

The Countess had now retired from Court to the country.

> Leaving the world before the world leaves thee;

and the Court, of which Emilia had been glad to breathe the air, if equivocally, is described as,

> That great enchantress of weak minds admired.

We come closer still to her in her invective against outward beauty unaccompanied by virtue — how well she knew it brought but dangers and disgrace!

> Who glories most, where most the danger lies ...
> For greatest perils do attend the fair
> When men do seek, attempt, plot and devise
> How they may overthrow the chastest Dame
> Whose beauty is the *white* whereat they aim.

She had not been the chastest of dames, we know, and had been aimed at for her dark beauty, her black hair, eyes and all. She had been taken advantage of by the Lord Chamberlain when hardly more than a girl; her father had died when she was young, leaving her on the world. If her personality, apart from her looks and undoubted talents, makes an unfavourable impression, we must reflect that she had had a raw deal. She was a strong personality, capable of putting men in their place, tough and resilient: she needed to be.

She cites examples of women who had been undone by their beauty — Helen of Troy, and Lucrece:

> 'Twas beauty made chaste Lucrece lose her life,
> For which proud Tarquin's fact was so abhorred.

Next Cleopatra and Antony. Shakespeare's play had been produced but a year or two before; Marlowe's friend, Edward Blount, entered it for publication in 1608, though it was not printed until after

Shakespeare's death, in the First Folio. Meanwhile Daniel had in 1607 re-published his *Tragedy of Cleopatra* with revisions for which he took some hints from Shakespeare's play. It is more likely that Emilia had Daniel in mind, for he was the poet of the Countess of Cumberland, his patron. Daniel lived quietly on the margin of this particular circle, addressing his Epistles not only to the Countess and her daughter, Lady Anne, but also to Southampton, Shakespeare's former patron and to Lord Chancellor Egerton, whom Emilia's husband had served. All these people were known to each other.

She goes on to cite Rosamund, whom Daniel had treated in the best of his *Complaints,* and Matilda, whom Drayton—Shakespeare's acquaintance and fellow Warwickshire man—had written about. Emilia herself was as well read as she was highly educated and talented. *Matilda* had been dedicated to the Countess of Bedford, to whom Daniel had written an Epistle and Emilia a poem.

She eschews popularity, however; she does not want the approbation of 'the Vulgar's breath' (which Shakespeare enjoyed as much as that of the sophisticated). She does not care for those of mean degree:

Mean minds will show of what mean moulds they be.

We see, again, that she has not ceased to be 'high-minded'; though reduced in status—that had always been equivocal, if elevated—she is still one of the elect few 'that wait on Poverty and Shame'. In the Passion of Christ she aligns herself with Pilate's 'most worthy wife', more worthy of respect than he was; however,

Let not us Women glory in Men's fall,
Who had power given to overrule us all.

This leads to an extended Apology for Eve, who is *less* to be blamed than Adam, for she was innocent and didn't know.

But surely Adam can not be excused,
Her fault though great, yet he was most to blame:
What Weakness offered, Strength might have refused ...

The attack on Adam is forcefully argued; one must pay tribute to Emilia's capacity for arguing in verse—a rather rare gift. No doubt she had a maddening way of having the last word—and what would John Milton have thought of her argument!

Adam had no business to lay the fault on Eve:

> That we (poor women) must endure it all ...
> No subtle serpent's falsehood did betray him,
> If he would eat it, who had power to stay him?

Not Eve, whose fault was only too much love. Besides, Adam owed knowledge to woman:

> Yet Men will boast of knowledge, which he took
> From Eve's fair hand ...

(Hadn't Shakespeare, always sympathetic to women, said as much years before in *Love's Labour's Lost*, in which Emilia was Rosaline, he Berowne:

> From women's eyes this doctrine I derive:
> They sparkle still the right Promethean fire;
> They are the books, the arts, the academes,
> That show, contain, and nourish all the world.

No doubt this sympathy of view had opened the way to his subjugation; a bisexual like Southampton was not so vulnerable, homosexuals like Marlowe, Bacon, James I, not at all.)

Emilia charges Adam with the responsibility for the Fall:

> he was the ground of all —
> If one of many worlds could lay a stain
> Upon our sex ...

Thereupon she raises her banner:

> Then let us have our Liberty again,
> And challenge to yourselves no sovereignty ...

Really, she might be a precursor of Women's Lib!

> You came not in the world without our pain,
> Make that a bar against your cruelty:
> Your fault being greater, why should you disdain
> Our being equals, free from tyranny?

We may observe, freely but consistently, that this was what the men-folk — the Lord Chamberlain who had discarded her, Alfonso who had taken her on unhappily, his actor-dramatist who had fallen for her, Forman who came to detest her — had all had to put up with. We may legitimately, if modestly, conclude that men found her a bit much.

Pontius Pilate had given way, in spite of his wiser wife's warnings, because he feared 'the People's threatenings'; no respect for 'the common sort' with the untitled lady (any more, for that matter, than with her former actor-lover). In a section, 'The teares of the daughters of Jerusalem', it was the women who had compassion on Christ (still nothing said about the Magdalen),

> When spiteful men with torments did oppress.

There follows a Hail Mary, with a tribute to the Virgin. We observe a few rare contemporary touches — would there were more! — 'the badges of like liveries' bespeaks the noble households she knew, 'a passing bell' rings a knell in our ears from Shakespeare; and we can appreciate her command of phrase in 'contrarieties contend'.

Odder, and perhaps more revealing, is her sensuous, not to say sexy, description of Christ. His 'cheeks washed with milk', his 'curlèd locks',

> Black as a raven in her blackest hue,
> His lips like scarlet threads, yet much more sweet ...

Suffice it to say that this is unlike the usual representations of him in the Renaissance and the Middle Ages, and that she herself had been praised by Shakespeare for her black beauty. Christ's lips are then described as 'like lilies' — it all makes a sensuous description of male

[28]

beauty, to which, for all her religiosity, it is nice to think that she was still responsive.

We pass over the religious persuasions to concentrate on personal indications, factual information as to her circle. The dowager Countess of Cumberland is handed the consolation that Christ proves 'by crosses and afflictions':

Yet still your heart remaineth firm and right;

the Countess has a 'constant soul', and doesn't respect riches or outward show; she rejects wealth and honour and place-seeking. She covers 'the stains of others' sins', to recover

Those weak lost sheep that did so long transgress:

here we have another oblique reflection of her own past—'in their conversion' Christ might behold something of her ladyship's worth and work. We note the snobbish thought that, had Christ

been but of a mean degree,
His sufferings had been small to what they were.

Then we are off to a longish consideration of the case of Antony and Cleopatra, which evidently made a strong impression on Emilia's mind (had she seen herself as Cleopatra, or had possibly the dramatist seen her as such?[1]), though her religious sympathies must be with chaste Octavia. A roll-call of famous women and their great deeds follows from classical and Biblical history. The Scythian women had put Darius to flight, even Alexander could not withstand their power. The deeds of Deborah, Judith, Esther, Susanna are next celebrated. The Countess is adjured that she 'needs no kinsman to advise'. For all that pious lady's contempt for wealth and honour, she pursued prolonged litigation with her late husband's brother and nephew, successors to the earldom, for what she could get of the inheritance for her

---

[1] This was the perceptive suggestion of Dame Agatha Christie in a letter to *The Times*.

daughter. Emilia says nothing of this, but pays tribute to her alms-giving—naturally enough, for she must have received some support from her.

Throughout the poem she is much concerned with Sin; like the preacher in the American story, she is now 'agin it'. 'Old doting Lust' is condemned, with 'unchaste desires', and 'desires of idle lovers'. The emphasis is now all on chastity. Perhaps by this time, at forty, Emilia had had enough of menfolk? It would seem so, and we must remind ourselves once again that her own experience could well have put her against men.

With Shakespeare—we should look at the affair from her point of view, which people never do. When the Sonnets began, in 1592, the impecunious actor, with wife and three children to support at Stratford, dependent on his patron for help, was twenty-eight, no longer young for an Elizabethan—indeed his life was more than half over. She was five years younger, at twenty-three; the young patron rising nineteen. What more natural than that, just out of the Lord Chamberlain's keeping, she should have seen a better bet in the young Lord than in his poet-actor? It is clear from the Sonnets how strongly and tempera-mentally she had reacted to being badgered by the older man who was conscious of being in a humiliating position, infatuated with a younger woman. When one knows the facts, and the ages of the three people involved, it all becomes so much more real and understandable.

In her long poem Emilia here makes a concession:

> Spirits affect where they do sympathise ...
> Beauty sometimes is pleased to feed her eyes
> With viewing Beauty in another's face:
> Both good and bad in this point do agree,
> That each desireth with his like to be.

Thus, too, the Queen of Sheba desired to set eyes on Solomon:

> Acting her glorious part upon a stage ...
> The world is but a stage where all do play their parts.

Cleopatra's love for Antony is not to be compared to the Countess's 'love divine'; *she* need have no fear of 'open shame'.

In taking leave of her subject, the Passion of Christ, 'a seeming tradesman's son', Emilia rounds up his martyrs, St Stephen, St Laurence, St Andrew, and hails the Countess as

> The Arctic star that guides my hand,
> All what I am, I rest at your command.

To the long religious poem Emilia appended 'The Description of Cooke-ham', where she had evidently passed happy summer days with the Countess and her daughter, Lady Anne, as a girl. The poem is in pentameter again, which Emilia falls into with natural ease, but this time in rhymed couplets. It provides a rare enough example of an Elizabethan topographical poem, with a rapturous response to the beauty of the landscape, if somewhat marred by a too prolonged example of the pathetic fallacy. Cookham Dean is evidently the place, up among hills and woods — when Emilia tells us that thirteen shires can be seen from it we recognise her tendency to exaggerate. In his last years the Earl and Countess of Cumberland lived separated: he fell in love with another woman, and was reconciled to his wife only on his deathbed in 1605. The injured wife left the Court and lived in the country, probably only temporarily at Cookham, where Emilia had been encouraged to write, by the

> Mistress of that place
> From whose desires did spring this work of Grace,

that is, the long religious poem.

We hear about the pleasures of the feminine life lived there, now over, the house graced with ornaments, the walks and woods in their summer liveries; walking together in the hills, the Countess with bow in hand, the favourite oak they often visited, placing the Bible in the tree to meditate or sing hymns; the Countess feeding the poor thereabouts. Then Lady Anne — to become so famous as an old woman in the North, having survived the next two Earls to succeed to the whole Clifford inheritance — was but a girl:

[31]

And that sweet Lady sprung from Clifford's race,
Of noble Bedfords' blood, fair stream of grace,
To honourable Dorset now espoused,
In whose fair breast true virtue then was housed:
Oh, what delight did my weak spirits find
In those pure parts of her well-framèd mind.

A no less characteristic note ensues:

And yet it grieves me that I cannot be
Near unto her ...
Unconstant Fortune, thou art most to blame,
Who casts us down into so low a frame,
Where our great friends we cannot daily see,
So great a difference is there of degree.

How very like Emilia, how consistent with all that we have learned of
her! She reflects:

Many are placèd in those orbs of state,
Parters in honour, so ordained by fate;
Nearer in show, yet farther off in love,
In which the lowest always are above.

Is that so, Emilia? It sounds more like a reproach, characteristic
resentment.

Formerly she had taken part in the entertainments of Cookham:

Remember beauteous Dorset's former sports —
So far from being touched by ill reports —
Wherein myself did always bear a part ...
Whereof deprived, I evermore must grieve,
Hating blind Fortune, careless to relieve.

Memory retained

Those pleasures past, which will not turn again ...
Where many a learned book was read and scanned,

[32]

and Anne Clifford would take her by the hand to their favourite tree, saying farewell to it with a chaste kiss. She ends with the desolation of the place when the ladies left, and

> This last farewell to Cookham here I give,
> When I am dead thy name in this may live.

Alas, it did not—one more reason for Emilia repining at her fate. Her book was received with stony silence. It may have achieved its purpose in reaping some reward from the dowager Countess—that would have been in keeping with current usage. But there is no evidence that any of the great ladies took any notice of the too obviously sycophantic poems with their clamorous assertions of virtue unrewarded, and hints to relieve. Few copies of the book can ever have been printed for so very few have survived.

ᴥ V ᴥ

Yet another law-suit throws a little more light on the Dark Lady's hitherto obscure career; once more it is completely consistent with what we have learned of her character, aggressive and clamorous, independent, restless and tough. The Chancery case she brought against a well known attorney, Edward Smith of Middle Temple, shows that in the summer of 1617 she took the lease of a house in St Giles in the Fields to set up a school.[1] The house had previously been occupied by Sir Edmond (or Edward) Morgan, who belonged to the Welsh clan of Lord Chamberlain Hunsdon's wife. Morgan was a professional, Low Countries soldier, one of Essex's many knights. The suburb was an aristocratic one. Among Emilia's neighbours were Sir Lewis Lewkenor, who had written a book on the English Catholic exiles in Spain, Sir Edward Fisher and Lady (Katherine) Cope.[2] Not

---

[1] C2/L11/64. James I. I am indebted for this reference to Miss Joyce Batty.
[2] E 179/142/279. I am grateful to Dr John Guy for this reference.

far away, at Holborn End, were still more grandees. Such a neighbour-
hood offered prospects for teaching the children of gentlefolk, and
Emilia should have felt at home. Nevertheless, forever discontented
with her lot—understandably after such beginnings—and querulous
as usual, she soon involved herself in a dispute.

It was about rent and repairs, £22 a year for one year 'if she
should like thereof'; if she did, then for another term of three years.
She deposed that she had been left in very poor estate by the death of
her husband, Captain Alfonso, 'he having spent a great part of her
estate in the service of the late Queen in her wars of Ireland and other
places', to the tune of £4000. This is simply incredible; she always
exaggerated and we do not believe her. Thus 'for her maintenance and
relief she was compelled to teach and educate the children of divers
persons of worth and understanding'—a characteristic touch. No doubt
she was well qualified to do so.

She claimed that she had spent £10 on repairs; and *en revanche* held
up payment of rent, according to the owner. Smith sent an agent who
told her 'with rude speeches' that he could find a better tenant, and
Morgan, who wished to return to the house, proceeded to dig up the
garden and plant trees without her consent. She stayed a year and a
half 'with continued trouble and molestation'; Smith could not get
her out, though he promised her another house. So he sued her in
the Court of Common Pleas for non-payment of rent, and arrested
her, 'a poor gentle-woman, in her own house'. This left 'your oratrix
and her children in great distress and want ... having taken upon her
the education of noblemen and gentlemen's children of great worth'—
there is the true Emilia note—'and she thereby greatly disgraced and
hindered'.

Smith's reply is more informative. He had spent £8 on repairing
the house, but 'did not know before that she depended on teaching
gentlemen's children and if that failed she would not be able to pay
the rent. As she was stark of payment of what she owes and therefore
not likely to pay the rent, he repented of his bargain and Sir Edmond
Morgan, who had lived in the house before, was very anxious to take

Shakespeare's Southampton
at the time of the Sonnets

Samuel Daniel

'Queen Elizabeth confounding the Goddesses'

it.' In the effort to persuade her to surrender the lease he offered to for-give her the first quarter's rent, but 'she very scornfully refused and said she would pay her rent as well as any Morgan in England'.

In fact she held on till August 1619, and then left without giving a quarter's notice and without paying her midsummer rent; upon which she was arrested. She had left the house, he said, 'in great decay, and in a nasty and filthy state.'

Perhaps that was but common form to plead; but what a come-down from her early, precarious height for poor Emilia! Nor can it have been pleasing to be dispossessed by Morgan, who had after all achieved a knighthood under Essex in Ireland, after all the hopes she had entertained of Alfonso's advancement.

After publishing her poem, with disappointing results, her life is one long drawn anti-climax. She went on so long — up to the end of the first Civil War — that I originally thought that there must be two Emilias. But no; it is the same old girl, Alfonso's widow, who went on to the exceptional age, for those days, of over seventy-six. She must have been as tough as she was litigious and tenacious, down on her luck but clamorous to the last.

Her son by the Lord Chamberlain was living in Clerkenwell when his daughter Mary was baptised on 25th July, 1627, and a son, another Henry, on 16th January, 1629.[1] On 29th September, 1629, Henry got a permanent post as one of the King's flautists,[2] but only four years later, on 14th October, 1633, he was buried at Clerkenwell. Two years later, 19th February, 1635, Emilia is petitioning in concern about Alfonso's monopoly of weighing hay and straw into London and Westminster.[3] She had agreed to make over her patent to her brother-in-law, Innocent Lanier, for him to obtain a new grant allowing her half the profits. She stated that she had received only £8, and was 'in great misery and having two grandchildren to provide for'. Hearing that suit had been made by others for the grant she

---

[1] *Registers of St James, Clerkenwell*, ed. R. Hovenden, i. 105, 113.
[2] H. C. de Lafontaine, *The King's Musick*, 70.
[3] *Cal. S.P. Dom., 1634–5*, 516.

prayed that the new patentee might pay her £50 out of the profits. This was opening her mouth rather wide.

Innocent had made over the grant to Clement Lanier. Charles I ordered Clement to pay her £20 a year, and after her decease £10 a year to the two grandchildren during the continuance of the grant. Next year, 1636, Emilia was petitioning again that endeavours had been made to serve Clement with the order; he had tendered her £4, requesting a general acquittance, swearing that he had great friends who would alter whatever the Privy Council had set down.[1] She prayed for £20 a year during the patent.

In May 1637 three witnesses testified on Clement's behalf that he had offered her £5 for Michaelmas and Lady Day quarters, which she had refused.[2] On 17th May, Clement put his case to the Council. Emilia had exhibited a bill in Chancery against him, and then withdrawn it to sue him *in forma pauperis* (as a poor person more advantageously) in the Court of Request.[3] The Court ordered him to pay her 20 nobles a year (a noble was 6s 8d, or 10s) until the hearing of the case—which he paid, but she never procured the cause to be heard. Instead, she had petitioned the Privy Council, which ordered him to pay £5 arrears and £10 yearly. He had paid her £5, and was willing to pay her £10 a year; 'but Emilia, not being satisfied with any of the same orders, preferred another petition' to the Privy Council obtaining £20 a year. This he is unable to pay because of the City's opposition to his grant.

The Council repeated its order of £5 arrears to Emilia up to May 1636; £10 a year thereafter for her maintenance and £10 after her decease to the grandchildren. If Clement Lanier recovered the full benefit of his grant—payments on which were collected at Smithfield and Puddlewharf—then he was to pay her £20 a year. We see the kind of vexations that were arising between the City of London and Charles I's government at Westminster—small pointers to the Civil

[1] *Cal. S.P. Dom., 1636–7*, 36.
[2] *Cal. S.P. Dom., 1736*, 71.
[3] Ibid., 115, 116.

War. In May next year, 1638, the Privy Council remonstrated with the Lord Mayor.[1] The King's servant, Clement Lanier, complained that, notwithstanding that he had spent £300 endeavouring to establish his grant, he was interrupted by directions from the Lord Mayor or Court of Aldermen. Unable to undergo suit at law with the City, he had petitioned the King, who commanded the Privy Council to settle the matter or report to him. They asked the Lord Mayor to take order so as 'his Majesty shall not be further troubled to interpose'.

We see the Civil War looming ahead. Emilia lived into it and through the first part of it, until she was buried on 3rd April, 1645 at Clerkenwell![2] She is described in the register as 'pensioner'—so she had managed to hold on to something to the last.

We must now leave her to speak for herself. It certainly is a most precious boon that we have been left this rare work by that extraordinary woman: in it we hear the acutely personal voice and read the character of Shakespeare's Dark Lady at last.

---

[1] *Cal. S.P. Dom., 1637–8*, 472.
[2] I owe this reference to Miss Mary Edmond.

SALVE DEVS

REX IVDÆORVM.

Containing,

1 The Pafsion of Chrift.

2 Eues Apologie in defence of Women.

3 The Teares of the Daughters of Ierufalem.

4 The Salutation and Sorrow of the Virgine Marie.

With diuers other things not vnfit to be read.

Written by Miftris *Æmilia Lanyer,* Wife to Captaine
Alfonfo Lanyer, Seruant to the
Kings Majeftie.

At LONDON

Printed by *Valentine Simmes* for *Richard Bonian,* and are
to be fold at his Shop in Paules Churchyard, at the
Signe of the Floure de Luce and
Crowne. 1611.

To the Queenes most
Excellent Majestie

Renowned Empresse, and great Britaines Queene,
Most gratious Mother of succeeding Kings;
Vouchsafe to view that which is seldome seene,
A Womans writing of divinest things:
 Reade it faire Queene, though it defective be,
 Your Excellence can grace both It and Mee.

For you have rifled Nature of her store,
And all the Goddesses have dispossest
Of those rich gifts which they enjoy'd before,
But now great Queene, in you they all doe rest.
 If now they strivèd for the golden Ball,
 Paris would give it you before them all.

From *Juno* you have State and Dignities,
From warlike *Pallas*, Wisdome, Fortitude;
And from faire *Venus* all her Excellencies,
With their best parts your Highnesse is indu'd :￬
 How much are we to honour those that springs
 From such rare beauty, in the blood of Kings?

The Muses doe attend upon your Throne,
With all the Artists at your becke and call;
The Sylvane Gods, and Satyres everyone,
Before your faire triumphant Chariot fall:
 And shining Cynthia with her nymphs attend
 To honour you, whose Honour hath no end.

From

From your bright spheare of greatnes where you sit,
Reflecting light to all those glorious stars
That wait upon your Throane; To virtue yet
Vouchsafe that splendor which my meannesse bars:
    Be like faire Phoebe, who doth love to grace
    The darkest night with her most beauteous face.

Apollo's beames doe comfort every creature,
And shines upon the meanest things that be;
Since in Estate and Virtue none is greater,
I humbly wish that yours may light on me:
    That so these rude unpolisht lines of mine,
    Graced by you, may seem the more divine.

Looke in this Mirrour of a worthy Mind,
Where some of your faire Virtues will appeare;
Though all is impossible to find,
Unlesse my Glasse were chrystall, or more cleare:
    Which is dim steele, yet full of spotlesse truth,
    And for one looke from your faire eyes it su'th.

Here may your sacred Majestie behold
That mightie Monarch both of heav'n and earth,
He that all Nations of the world controld,
Yet tooke our flesh in base and meanest berth:
    Whose daies were spent in poverty and sorrow,
    And yet all Kings their wealth of him do borrow.

For he is Crowne and Crowner of all Kings,
The hopeful haven of the meaner sort,
Its he that all our ioyfull tidings brings
Of happie raigne within his royall Court:
    Its he that in extremity can give
    Comfort to them that have no time to live.

And

And since my wealth within his Region stands,
And that his Crosse my chiefest comfort is,
Yea in his kingdome onely rests my lands,
Of honour there I hope I shall not misse:
 Though I on earth doe live unfortunate,
 Yet there I may attaine a better state.

In the meane time, accept most gratious Queene
This holy worke, Virtue presents to you,
In poore apparell, shaming to be seene,
Or once t'appeare in your judiciall view:
 But that faire Virtue, though in meane attire,
 All Princes of the world doe most desire.

And sith all royall virtues are in you,
The Naturall, the Morall, and Divine,
I hope how plaine soever, beeing true,
You will accept even of the meanest line
 Faire Virtue yeelds; by whose rare gifts you are
 So highly graced, t'exceed the fairest faire.

Behold, great Queene, faire *Eves* Apologie,
Which I have writ in honour of your sexe,
And doe referre unto your Majestie,
To judge if it agree not with the Text:
 And if it doe, why are poore Women blam'd,
 Or by more faultie Men so much defam'd?

And this great Lady I have here attired,
In all her richest ornaments of Honour,
That you faire Queene, of all the world admired,
May take the more delight to looke upon her:
 For she must entertaine you to this Feast,
 To which your Highnesse is the welcom'st guest.

For

For here I have prepar'd my Paschal Lambe,
The figure of that living Sacrifice;
Who dying, all th'Infernall powres oercame,
That we with him t'Eternitie might rise:
  This pretious Passeover feed upon, O Queene,
  Let your faire Virtues in my Glasse be seene.

The Lady And she that is the patterne of all Beautie,
Elizabeths The very modell of your Majestie,
Grace   Whose rarest parts enforceth Love and Duty,
    The perfect patterne of all Pietie:
     O let my Booke by her faire eies be blest,
     In whose pure thoughts all Innocency rests.

Then shall I thinke my Glasse a glorious Skie,
When two such glittring Suns at once appeare;
The one repleat with Sov'raigne Majestie,
Both shining brighter than the clearest cleare:
  And both reflecting comfort to my spirits,
  To find their grace so much above my merits

Whose untun'd voyce the dolefull notes doth sing
Of sad Affliction in an humble straine;
Much like unto a Bird that wants a wing,
And cannot flie, but warbles forth her paine:
  Or he that barred from the Suns bright light,
  Wanting daies comfort, doth comend the night.

So that I live clos'd up in Sorrowes Cell,
Since great *Elizaes* favour blest my youth;
And in the confines of all cares doe dwell,
Whose grieved eyes no pleasure ever view'th:
  But in Christs suffrings, such sweet taste they have,
  As makes me praise pale Sorrow and the Grave.

And

And this great Ladie whom I love and honour,
And from my very tender yeeres have knowne,
This holy habite still to take upon her,
Still to remain *the same*, and still her owne:
    And what our fortunes doe enforce us to,
    She of Devotion and meere Zeale doth do.

Which makes me thinke our heavy burden light,
When such a one as she will help to beare it:
Treading the paths that make our way go right,
What garment is so faire but she may weare it;
    Especially for her that entertaines
    A Glorious Queene, in whome all woorth remains.

Whose powre may raise my sad dejected Muse,
From this lowe Mansion of a troubled mind;
Whose princely favour may such grace infuse,
That I may spread Her Virtues in like kind:
    But in this triall of my slender skill,
    I wanted knowledge to performe my will.

For even as they that doe behold the Starres,
Not with the eie of Learning, but of Sight,
To find their motions, want of knowledge barres
Although they see them in their brightest light:
    So, though I see the glory of her State,
    Its she that must instruct and elevate.

My weake distempred braine and feeble spirits,
Which all unlearned have adventur'd, this
To write of Christ, and of his sacred merits,
Desiring that this Booke Her hands may kisse:
    And though I be unworthy of that grace,
    Yet let her blessed thoghts this book imbrace.

And

And pardon me (faire Queene) though I presume,
To doe that which so many better can;
Not that I Learning to my selfe assume,
Or that I would compare with any man:
    But as they are Scholers, and by Art do write,
    So Nature yeelds my Soule a sad delight.

And since all Arts at first from Nature came,
That goodly Creature, Mother of perfection,
Whom *Joves* almighty hand at first did frame,
Taking both her and hers in his protection:
    Why should not She now grace my barren Muse,
    And in a Woman all defects excuse.

So peerelesse Princesse humbly I desire,
That your great wisedome would vouchsafe t'omit
All faults; and pardon if my spirits retire,
Leaving to ayme at what they cannot hit:
    To write your worth, which no pen can expresse,
    Were but t'ecclipse your Fame, and make it lesse.

To

To the Lady Elizabeths
Grace

Most gratious Ladie, faire Elizabeth,
    Whose Name and Virtues puts us still in mind,
    Of her, of whom we are depriv'd by death;
The *Phoenix* of her age, whose worth did bind
All worthy minds so long as they have breath,
    In linkes of admiration, love and zeale,
    To that deare Mother of our Common-weale.

Even you faire Princesse next our famous Queene,
I doe invite unto this wholesome feast,
Whose goodly wisedome, though your yeares be greene
By such good workes may daily be increast,
Though your fair eyes farre better Bookes have seene;
    Yet being the first fruits of a womans wit,
    Vouchsafe you favour in accepting it.

To

To all vertuous Ladies in generall.

Each blessed Lady that in Virtue spends
Your pretious time to beautifie your soules;
Come wait on hir whom winged Fame attends
And in hir hand the Booke where she inroules
Those high deserts that Majestie commends:
    Let this faire Queene not unattended bee,
    When in my Glasse she daines her selfe to see.

Put on your wedding garments every one,
The Bridegroome stayes to entertaine you all;
Let Virtue be your guide, for she alone
Can leade you right that you can never fall;
And make no stay for feare he should be gone:
    But fill your Lamps with oyle of burning zeale,
    That to your Faith he may his truth reveale.

Let all your roabes be purple scarlet white,
Those perfit colours purest Virtue wore,
Come deckt with Lillies that did so delight
To be preferr'd in Beauty, farre before
Wise *Salomon* in all his glory dight:
    Whose royall roabes did no such pleasure yield,
    As did the beauteous Lilly of the field

*The roabes
that Christ
wore before
his death*

Adorne

To all virtuous Ladies in generall

In token of
Constancie

Adorne your temples with faire *Daphnes* crowne,
The never changing Laurel, alwaies greene;
Let constant hope all worldly pleasures drowne,
In wise *Minervaes* paths be alwaies seene;
Or with bright *Cynthia*, thogh faire *Venus* frown:
  With *Esop* crosse the posts of every doore,
  Where Sinne would riot, making Virtue poore.

And let the Muses your companions be,
Those sacred sisters that on *Pallas* wait;
Whose Virtues with the purest minds agree,
Whose godly labours doe avoyde the baite
Of worldly pleasures, living alwaies free
  From sword, from violence, and from ill report,
  To these nine Worthies all faire mindes resort.

Annoynt your haire with *Aarons* pretious oyle,
And bring your palmes of vict'ry in your hands,
To overcome all thoughts that would defile
The earthly circuit of your soules faire lands;
Let no dimme shadowes your cleare eyes beguile:
  Sweet odours, mirrhe, gum, aloes, frankincense,
  Present that King who di'd for your offence.

Behold, bright *Titans* shining chariot staies,
All deckt with flowers of the freshest hew,
Attended on by Age, Houres, Nights, and Daies,
Which alters not your beauty, but gives you
Much more, and crownes you with eternall praise:
  This golden chariot wherein you must ride,
  Let simple Doves, and subtill serpents guide.

Come

To all virtuous Ladies in generall

Come swifter than the motion of the Sunne,
To be transfigur'd with our loving Lord,
Lest Glory end what Grace in you begun,
Of heav'nly riches make your greatest hoord,
In Christ all honour, wealth and beautie's wonne:
    By whose perfections you appeare more faire
    Than *Phoebus*, if he seav'n times brighter were.

Gods holy Angels will direct your Doves,
And bring your Serpents to the fields of rest,
Where he doth stay that purchast all your loves
In bloody torments, when he di'd opprest,
There shall you find him in those pleasant groves
    Of sweet *Elizium*, by the Well of Life,
    Whose cristal springs do purge from worldly strife.

Thus may you flie from dull and sensuall earth,
Whereof at first your bodies formed were,
That new regen'rate in a second berth
Your blessed soules may live without all feare,
Beeing immortall, subject to no death:
    But in the eie of heaven so highly placed
    That others by your virtues may be graced.

Where worthy Ladies I will leave you all,
Desiring you to grace this little Booke;
Yet some of you me thinkes I heare to call
Me by my name, and bid me better looke,
Lest unawares I in an error fall:
    In generall tearmes, to place you with the rest,
    Whom Fame commends to be the very best.

Tis

Queen Anne, James I's Queen

Lady Arabella Stuart

To all virtuous Ladies in generall

Tis true, I must confesse (O noble Fame)
There are a number honoured by thee,
Of which, some few thou didst recite by name,
And willd my Muse they should remembred bee;
Wishing some would their glorious Trophies frame:
    Which if I should presume to undertake,
    My tired Hand for very feare would quake.

Onely by name I will bid some of those,
That in true Honors seate have long bin placed,
Yea even such as thou hast chiefly chose,
By whom my Muse may be the better graced;
Therefore, unwilling longer time to lose,
    I will invite some Ladies that I know,
    But chiefly those as thou hast graced so.

To

To the Ladie Arabella

Great learned Ladie, whom I long have knowne,
And yet not knowne so much as I desired:
Rare *Phoenix*, whose faire feathers are your owne,
With which you flie, and are so much admired:
True honour whom true Fame hath so attired,
  In glittering raiment shining much more bright,
  Than silver Starres in the most frostie night.

Come like the morning Sunne new out of bed,
And cast your eyes upon this little Booke,
Although you be so well accompan'ed
With *Pallas*, and the Muses, spare one looke
Upon this humbled King, who all forsooke,
  That in his dying armes he might imbrace
  Your beauteous Soule, and fill it with his grace.

To the Ladie Susan,
Countesse Dowager of Kent, and daughter to the Duchesse of Suffolke.

Come you that were the Mistris of my youth,
   The noble guide of my ungovern'd dayes;
   Come you that have delighted in Gods truth,
Help now your handmaid to sound foorth his praise:
     You that are pleas'd in his pure excellencie,
     Vouchsafe to grace this holy feast, and me.

And as your rare Perfections shew'd the Glasse
Wherein I saw each wrinckle of a fault;
You the Sunnes virtue, I that faire greene grasse,
That flourisht fresh by your cleere virtues taught:
     For you possest those gifts that grace the mind,
     Restraining youth whom Errour oft doth blind.

In you these noble Virtues did I note,
First, love and feare of God, of Prince, of Lawes,
Rare Patience with a mind so farre remote
From worldly pleasures, free from giving cause
     Of least suspect to the most envious eie,
     That in faire Virtues Storehouse sought to prie.

Whose Faith did undertake in Infancie,
All dang'rous travells by devouring Seas
To flie to Christ from vaine Idolatry,
Not seeking there this worthlesse world to please,
     By your most famous Mother so directed,
     That noble Dutchesse, who liv'd unsubjected.

From

From *Romes* ridiculous prier and tyranny,
That mighty Monarchs kept in awfull feare;
Leaving here her lands, her state, dignitie;
Nay more, vouchsaft disguised weedes to weare:
    When with Christ Jesus she did meane to goe,
    From sweet delights to taste part of his woe.

Come you that ever since hath followed her,
In these sweet paths of faire Humilitie;
Contemning Pride pure Virtue to preferre,
Not yielding to base Imbecillitie,
    Nor to those weake inticements of the world,
    That have so many thousand Soules insnarld.

Receive your Love whom you have sought so farre,
Which heere presents himselfe within your view;
Behold this bright and all directing Starre,
Light of your Soule that doth all grace renew:
    And in his humble paths since you do tread,
    Take this faire Bridegroome in your soules pure bed.

And since no former gaine hath made me write,
Nor my desertlesse service could have wonne,
Onely your noble Virtues do incite
My Pen, they are the ground I write upon;
    Nor any future profit is expected,
    Then how can these poor lines go unrespected?

                        The

The Authors Dreame to the Ladie Marie, the Countesse Dowager of Pembroke.

Me thought I pass'd through th' *Edalyan* Groves,
And askt the Graces, if they could direct
Me to a Lady whom *Minerva* chose,
To live with her in height of all respect.

Yet looking backe into my thoughts againe,
The eie of Reason did behold her there
Fast ti'd unto them in a golden Chaine,
They stood, but she was set in Honors chaire.

And nine faire Virgins sate upon the ground,
With Harps and Vialls in their lilly hands;
Whose harmony had all my sences drown'd,
But that before mine eyes an object stands,

Whose Beauty shin'd like *Titons* cleerest raies,
She blew a brazen Trumpet, which did sound
Throgh al the world that worthy Ladies praise,
And by Eternall Fame I saw her crown'd.

Yet studying, if I were awake, or no,
God *Morphy* came and tooke me by the hand,
And wil'd me not from Slumbers bowre to go,   *The God of*
Till I the summe of all did understand.   *Dreames*

When

[55]

When presently the Welkin that before
Look'd bright and cleere, me thought, was overcast,
And duskie clouds, with boyst'rous winds great store,
Foretold of violent stormes which could not last.

And gazing up into the troubled skie,
Me thought a Chariot did from thence descend,
Where one did sit repleat with Majestie,
Drawne by foure fierie Dragons, which did bend

Their course where this most noble Lady sate,
Whom all these virgins with due reverence
Did entertaine, according to that state
Which did belong unto her Excellence.

Goddesse of
Warre and
Wisdome

When bright *Bellona*, so they did her call,
Whom these faire Nymphs so humbly did receive,
A manly maid which was both faire and tall,
Her borrowed Charret by a spring did leave.

With speare, and shield, and currat on her breast,
And on her head a helmet wondrous bright,
With myrtle, bayes, and olive branches drest,
Wherein me thought I tooke no small delight

To see how all the Graces sought grace here,
And in what meeke, yet princely sort she came;
How this most noble Lady did imbrace her,
And all humors unto hers did frame.

Now

Now faire *Dictina* by the breake of Day,   *The Moone*
With all her Damsels round about her came,
Ranging the woods to hunt, yet made a stay,
When harkning to the pleasing sound of Fame;

Her Ivory bowe and silver shaftes shee gave
Unto the fairest nymphe of all her traine;
And wondring who it was that in so grave,
Yet gallant fashion did her beauty staine:

Shee deckt her selfe with all the borrowed light
That *Phoebus* would afford from his faire face,
And made her Virgins to appeare so bright,
That all the hils and vales received grace.

Then pressing where this beauteous troupe did stand,
They all received her most willingly,
And unto her the Lady gave her hand,
That shee should keepe with them continually.

Aurora rising from her rosie bedde,   *The*
First blusht, then wept, to see faire *Phoebe* grac'd,   *Morning*
And unto Lady *Maie* these wordes shee sed,
Come, let us goe, we will not be out-fac'd.

I will unto *Apolloes* Waggoner,
A bidde him bring his Master presently,
That his bright beames may all her Beauty marre,
Gracing us with the luster of his eie.

                                        Come,

Come, come, sweet Maie, and fill their laps with floures,
And I will give a greater light than she:
So all these Ladies favours shall be ours,
None shall be more esteem'd than we shall be.

Thus did *Aurora* dimme faire *Phoebus* light,
And was receiv'd in bright *Cynthiaes* place,
While *Flora* all with fragrant floures dight,
Pressed to shew the beauty of her face.

Though these, me thought, were verie pleasing sights,
Yet now these Worthies did agree to go,
Unto a place full of all rare delights,
A place that yet *Minerva* did not know.

That sacred Spring where Art and Nature striv'd
Which should remaine as Sov'raigne of the place,
Whose antient quarrel being new reviv'd,
Added fresh Beauty, gave farre greater Grace.

To which as umpiers now these Ladies go,
Judging with pleasure their delightfull case;
Whose ravisht sences made them quickely know,
'Twould be offensive either to displace.

And therefore will'd they should for ever dwell,
In perfit unity by this matchlesse Spring:
Since 'twas impossible either should excell,
Or her faire fellow in subjection bring.

But

But here in equal sov'raigntie to live,
Equall in state, equall in dignitie,
That unto others they might comfort give,
Rejoycing all with their sweet unitie.

And now me thought I long to heare her name,
Whom wise *Minerva* honoured so much,
Shee whom I saw was crownd by noble Fame,
Whom Envy sought to sting, yet could not tuch.

Me thought the meager elfe did seeke bie waies
To come unto her, but it would not be;
Her venime purifi'd by virtues raies,
Shee pin'd and starv'd like an Anotomie:

While beauteous *Pallas* with this Lady faire,
Attended by these Nymphs of noble fame,
Beheld those woods, those groves, those bowers rare,
By which *Pergusa*, for so hight the name

Of that faire spring, his dwelling place and ground;
And throgh those fields with sundry flowers clad,
Of sev'rall colours, to adorne the ground,
And please the sences ev'n of the most sad:

He trayld along the woods in wanton wise,
With sweet delight to entertaine them all;
Inviting them to sit and to devise
On holy hymnes; at last to mind they call

Those

The Psalms
written newly
by the
Countesse
Dowager of
Penbrooke

Those rare sweet songs which *Israels* King did frame
Unto the Father of Eternitie;
Before his holy wisedom tooke the name
Of great *Messias*, Lord of unitie.

Those holy Sonnets they did all agree,
With this most lovely Lady here to sing;
That by her noble breasts sweet harmony,
Their musicke might in eares of Angels ring.

While saints like Swans about this silver brook
Should Hallalu-iah sing continually,
Writing her praises in th'eternall booke
Of endlesse honour, true fames memorie.

Thus I in sleep the heavenli'st musicke hard,
That ever earthly eares did entertaine;
And durst not wake, for feare to be debard
Of what my sences sought still to retaine.

Yet sleeping, praid dull Slumber to unfold
Her noble name, who was of all admired;
When presently in drowsie tearmes he told
Not onely that, but more than I desired.

This nymph, quoth he, great *Penbrooke* hight by name,
Sister to valiant *Sidney*, whose cleere light
Gives light to all that tread true paths of Fame,
Who in the globe of heav'n doth shine so bright;

That

That beeing dead, his fame doth him survive,
Still living in the hearts of worthy men;
Pale Death is dead, but he remaines alive,
Whose dying wounds restor'd him life agen.

And this faire earthly goddesse which you see,
Bellona and her virgins doe attend;
In virtuous studies of Divinitie,
Her pretious time continually doth spend.

So that a Sister well shee may be deemd,
To him that liv'd and di'd so nobly;
And farre before him is to be esteemed
For virtue, wisedome, learning, dignity.

Whose beauteous soule hath gain'd a double life,
Both here on earth, and in the heav'ns above,
Till dissolution end all worldly strife:
Her blessed spirit remaines, of holy love,

Directing all by her immortall light,
In this huge sea of sorrowes, griefes, and feares;
With contemplation of Gods powrefull might,
Shee fils the eies, the hearts, the tongues, the eares

Of after-comming ages, which shall reade
Her love, her zeale, her faith and pietie;
The faire impression of whose worthy deed,
Seales her pure soule unto the Deitie.

That

That both in Heav'n and Earth it may remaine,
Crownd with her Makers glory and his love;
And this did Father Slumber tell with paine,
Whose dulnesse scarce could suffer him to move.

When I awaking left him and his bowre,
Much grieved that I could no longer stay;
Sencelesse was sleepe, not to admit me powre,
As I had spent the night to spend the day:

Then had God *Morphie* shew'd the end of all,
And what my heart desir'd, mine eies had seene;
For as I wak'd me thought I heard one call
For that bright Charet lent by *Joves* faire Queene.

To Sleepe

But thou, base cunning thiefe, that robs our sprits
Of halfe that span of life which yeares doth give;
And yet no praise unto thy selfe it merits,
To make a seeming death in those that live.

Yea wickedly thou doest consent to death,
Within thy restful bed to rob our soules;
In Slumbers bowre thou steal'st away our breath,
Yet none there is that thy base stealths controules.

If poore and sickly creatures would imbrace thee,
Or they to whom thou giv'st a taste of pleasure,
Thou fli'st as if *Acteons* hounds did chase thee,
Or that to stay with them thou hadst no leasure.

But

But though thou hast depriv'd me of delight,
By stealing from me ere I was aware;
I know I shall enjoy the selfe same sight,
Thou hast no powre my waking sprites to barre.

For to this Lady now I will repaire,
Presenting her the fruits of idle houres;
Thogh many Books she writes that are more rare,
Yet there is honey in the meanest flowres:

Which is both wholesome, and delights the taste:
Though sugar be more finer, higher priz'd,
Yet is the painefull Bee no whit disgrac'd,
Nor her faire wax, or hony more despiz'd.

And though that learned damsel and the rest,
Have in a higher style her Trophie fram'd;
Yet these unlearned lines beeing my best,
Of her great wisedom can no whit be blam'd.

And therefore, first I here present my Dreame,
And next, invite her Honour to my feast;
For my clear reason sees her by that streame,
Where her rare virtues daily are increast.

So craving pardon for this bold attempt,
I here present my mirrour to her view,
Whose noble virtues cannot be exempt,
My Glasse beeing steele, declares them to be true.

And

And Madame, if you will vouchsafe that grace,
To grace those flowres that springs from virtues ground;
Though your faire mind on worthier workes is plac'd,
On workes that are more deepe, and more profound;

Yet is it no disparagement to you,
To see your Saviour in a Shepheards weed,
Unworthily presented in your viewe,
Whose worthinesse will grace each line you reade.

Receive him here by my unworthy hand,
And reade his paths of faire humility;
Who though our sinnes in number passe the sand,
They are all purged by his Divinity.

To

To the Lady Lucie, Countesse of Bedford

Me thinkes I see faire Virtue readie stand,
T'unlocke the closet of your lovely breast,
Holding the key of Knowledge in her hand,
Key of that Cabbine where your selfe doth rest,
To let him in, by whom her youth was blest.
    The true-love of your soule, your hearts delight,
    Fairer than all the world in your cleare sight.

He that descended from celestiall glory,
To taste of our infirmities and sorrowes,
Whose heavenly wisdom read the earthly storie
Of fraile Humanity, which his godhead borrows:
Loe here he coms all stucke with pale deaths arrows:
    In whose most pretious wounds your soule may reade
    Salvation, while he (dying Lord) doth bleed.

You whose cleare Judgement farre exceeds my skil,
Vouchsafe to entertain this dying lover,
The Ocean of true grace, whose streames doe fill
All those with Joy, that can his love recover;
About this blessed Arke bright Angels hover:
    Where your faire soule may sure and safely rest,
    When he is sweetly seated in your breast.

There may your thoughts as servants to your heart,
Give true attendance on this lovely guest,
While he doth to that blessed bowre impart
Flowres of fresh comforts, decke that bed of rest,
With such rich beauties as may make it blest:
    And you in whom all raritie is found,
    May be with his eternall glory crownd.

To

To the Ladie Margaret, Countesse Dowager of Cumberland

Right Honourable and Excellent Lady, I may say with Saint Peter, *Silver nor gold have I none, but such as I have, that give I you*: for having neither rich pearles of India, nor fine gold of Arabia, nor diamonds of inestimable value; neither those rich treasures, Arramaticall Gums, incense, and sweet odours, which were presented by those Kingly Philosophers to the babe Jesus, I present unto you even our Lord Jesus himselfe, whose infinit value is not to be comprehended within the weake imagination or wit of man: and as Saint *Peter* gave health to the body, so I deliver you the health of the soule; which is this most pretious pearle of all perfection, this rich diamond of devotion, this perfect gold growing in the veines of that excellent earth of the most blessed Paradice, wherein our second *Adam* had his restlesse habitation. The sweet incense, balsums, odours, and gummes that flowes from that beautifull tree of Life, sprung from the roote of *Jessie*, which is so super-excellent, that it giveth grace to the meanest and most unworthy hand that will undertake to write thereof; neither can it receive any blemish thereby: for as a right diamond can loose no whit of his beautie by the blacke soyle underneath it, neither by beeing placed in the darke, but retaines his naturall beauty and brightnesse shining in greater perfection than before; so this most pretious diamond, for beauty and riches exceeding all the most pretious diamonds and rich jewels of the world, can receive no blemish, nor impeachment by

my

Susan Bertie, Countess of Kent

Mary Sidney, Countess of Pembroke

my unworthy hand writing; but wil with the Sunne retaine
his owne brightnesse and most glorious lustre, though never so many blind eyes looke upon him. Therefore good
Madame, to the most perfect eyes of your understanding, I
deliver the inestimable treasure of all elected soules, to bee
perused at convenient times; as also the mirrour of your
most worthy minde, which may remaine in the world many yeares longer than your Honour, or my selfe can live, to
be a light unto those that come after, desiring to tread in the
narrow path of virtue, that leads the way to heaven. In
which way, I pray God send your Honour long to continue, that your light may so shine before men, that they may
glorifie your father which is in Heaven: and that I and many others may follow you in the same tracke. So wishing
you in this world all increase of health and honour, and in
the world to come life everlasting, I rest.

To the Ladie Katherine, Countesse of Suffolke

Although great Lady, it may seeme right strange,
That I a stranger should presume thus farre,
To write to you; yet as the times doe change,
So are we subject to that fatall starre,
 Under the which we were produc'd to breath,
 That starre that guides us even untill our death.

And guided me to frame this worke of grace,
Not of it selfe, but by celestiall powres,
To which, both that and wee must needs give place,
Since what we have, we cannot count it ours:
 For health, wealth, honour, sickenesse, death and all,
 Is in Gods powre, which makes us rise and fall.

And since his powre hath given me powre to write,
A subject fit for you to looke upon,
Wherein your soule may take no small delight,
When her bright eyes beholds that holy one:
 By whose great wisedome, love, and speciall grace,
 Shee was created to behold his face.

Vouchsafe sweet Lady, to accept these lines,
Writ by a hand that doth desire to doe
All services to you whose worth combines
The worthi'st minds to love and honour you:
 Whose beautie, wisedome, children, high estate,
 Doe all concurre to make you fortunate.

But

But chiefly your most honourable Lord,
Whose noble virtues Fame can ne'er forget:
His hand being alwayes ready to afford
Help to the weake, to the unfortunate:
 All which begets more honour and respect,
 Than *Croessus* wealth, or *Caesars* sterne aspect.

And rightly sheweth that hee is descended
Of honourable *Howards* antient house,
Whose noble deedes by former times commended,
Do now remaine in your most loyall Spouse,
 On whom God powres all blessings from above,
 Wealth, honour, children and a worthy Love;

Which is more deare to him than all the rest,
You being the loving Hinde and pleasant Roe,
Wife of his youth, in whom his soule is blest,
Fountaine from whence his chiefe delights do flow.
 Faire tree from which the fruit of Honor springs,
 Heere I present to you the King of kings:

Desiring you to take a perfit view,
Of those great torments Patience did indure;
And reape those Comforts that belongs to you,
Which his most painful death did then assure:
 Writing the Covenant with his pretious blood,
 That your faire soule might bathe her in that flood.

And let your noble daughters likewise reade
This little Booke that I present to you;
On heavenly food let them vouchsafe to feede;
Heere they may see a Lover much more true
 Than ever was since first the world began,
 This poore rich King that di'd both God and man.

             Yea,

Yea, let those Ladies which do represent
All beauty, wisedome, zeale, and love,
Receive this jewell from *Jehova* sent,
This spotless Lambe, this perfit patient Dove:
    Of whom faire *Gabriel*, Gods bright *Mercury*,
    Brought downe a message from the Deitie.

Here may they see him in a flood of teares,
Crowned with thornes, and bathing in his blood;
Here may they see his feares exceed all feares,
When Heaven in Justice flat against him stood:
    And loathsome death with grim and gastly look,
    Presented him that blacke infernall booke,

Wherein the sinnes of all the world were writ,
In deepe Characters of due punishment;
And naught but dying breath could cancel it:
Shame, death, and hell must make the attonement:
    Shewing their evidence, seizing wrongful Right,
    Placing heav'ns Beauty in deaths darkest night.

Yet through the sable Clowdes of Shame and Death,
His beauty shewes more clearer than before;
Death lost his strength when he did loose his breath:
As fire supprest doth shine and flame the more,
    So in Deaths ashie pale discoloured face,
    Fresh beauty shin'd, yeelding farre greater grace.

No Dove, no Swan, nor Iv'rie could compare
With this faire corps, when 'twas by death imbrac'd;
No rose, nor no vermillion halfe so faire
As was that pretious blood that interlac'd
    His body, which bright Angels did attend,
    Waiting on him that must to Heaven ascend.

In

In whom is all that Ladies can desire;
If Beauty, who hath bin more faire than he?
If Wisedome, doth not all the world admire
The depth of his, that cannot searched be?
    If wealth, if honour, fame or Kingdoms store,
    Who ever liv'd that was possest of more?

If zeale, if grace, if love, if pietie,
If constancie, if faith, if faire obedience,
If valour, patience, or sobrietie;
If chast behaviour, meekenesse, continence,
    If justice, mercie, bountie, charitie,
    Who can compare with his Divinitie?

Whose vertues more than thoughts can apprehend,
I leave to their more cleere imagination,
That will vouchsafe their borrowed time to spend
In meditating, and in contemplation
    Of his rare parts, true honours faire prospect,
    The perfect line that goodnesse doth direct.

And unto you I wish those sweet desires,
That from your perfect thoughts doe daily spring,
Increasing still pure, bright, and holy fires,
Which sparkes of pretious grace, by faith doe spring:
    Mounting your soule unto eternall rest,
    There to live happily among the best.

                           To

To the Ladie Anne, Countesse of Dorcet

To you I dedicate this worke of Grace,
This frame of Glory which I have erected,
For your faire mind I hold the fittest place,
Where virtue should be setled and protected;
If highest thoughts true honor do imbrace,
And holy Wisdom if of them respected:
    Then in this Mirrour let your faire eyes looke,
    To view your virtues in this blessed Booke.

Blest by our Saviours merits, not my skil,
Which I acknowledge to be very small;
Yet if the least part of his blessed Will
I have perform'd, I count I have done all:
One sparke of grace sufficient is to fill
Our Lampes with oyle, ready when he doth call
    To enter with the Bridegroome to the feast,
    Where he that is the greatest may be least.

Greatnesse is no sure frame to build upon,
No worldly treasure can assure that place;
God makes both even, the Cottage with the Throne,
All worldly honours there are counted base;
Those he holds deare, and reckneth as his owne,
Whose virtuous deeds by his especially grace
    Have gain'd his love, his kingdome, and his crowne,
    Whom in the booke of Life he hath set downe.

Titles

Titles of honour which the world bestowes,
To none but to the virtuous doth belong;
As beauteous bowres where true worth should repose,
And where his dwelling should be built most strong:
But when they are bestow'd upon her foes,
Poore virtues friends indure the greatest wrong:
    For they must suffer all indignity,
    Untill in heav'n they better graced be.

What difference was there when the world began,
Was it not Virtue that distinguisht all?
All sprang but from one woman and one man,
Then how doth Gentry come to rise and fall?
Or who is he that very rightly can
Distinguish of his birth, or tell at all
    In what meane state his Ancestors have bin,
    Before some one of worth did honour win?

Whose successors, although they beare his name,
Possessing not the riches of his minde,
How doe we know they spring out of the same
True stocke of honour, beeing not of that kind?
It is faire virtue gets immortall fame,
Tis that doth all love and duty bind:
    If he that much enjoyes, doth little good,
    We may suppose he comes not of that blood.

Nor is he fit for honour, or command,
If base affections over-rules his mind;
Or that selfe-will doth carry such a hand,
As worldly pleasures have the powre to blind
So as he cannot see, nor understand
How to discharge that place to him assign'd:
    Gods Stewards must for all the poore provide,
    If in Gods house they purpose to abide.

To

To you, as to Gods Steward I doe write,
In whom the seeds of virtue have bin sowne,
By your most worthy mother, in whose right,
All her faire parts you challenge as your owne;
If you, sweet Lady, will appeare as bright
As ever creature did that time hath knowne,
 Then weare this Diadem I present to thee,
 Which I have fram'd for her Eternitie.

You are the Heire apparent of this Crowne
Of goodnesse, bountie, grace, love, pietie,
By birth its yours, then keepe it as your owne,
Defend it from all base indignitie;
The right your Mother hath to it, is knowne
Best unto you, who reapt such fruit thereby:
 This Monument of her faire worth retaine
 In your pure mind, and keepe it from al staine.

And as your Ancestors at first possest
Their honours, for their honourable deeds,
Let their faire virtues never be transgrest,
Bind up the broken, stop the wounds that bleeds,
Succour the poore, comfort the comfortlesse,
Cherish faire plants, suppress unwholsom weeds;
 Although base pelfe do chance to come in place,
 Yet let true worth receive your greatest grace.

So shal you shew from whence you are descended,
And leave to all posterities your fame,
So will your virtues alwaies be commended,
And every one will reverence your name;
So this poore worke of mine shalbe defended
From any scandal that the world can frame:
 And you a glorious Actor will appeare
 Lovely to all, but unto God most deare.

I know

I know right well these are but needlesse lines,
To you, that are so perfect in your part,
Whose birth and education both combines;
Nay more than both, a pure and godly heart,
So well instructed to such faire designes,
By your deere Mother, that there needs no art:
        Your ripe discretion in your tender yeares,
        By all your actions to the world appeares.

I doe but set a candle in the sunne,
And adde one drop of water to the sea,
Virtue and Beautie both together run,
When you were borne, within your breast to stay;
Their quarrel ceast, which long before begun,
They live in peace, and all doe them obey:
        In you faire Madame, are they richly plac'd,
        Where all their worth by Eternity is grac'd.

You goddesse-like unto the world appeare,
Inricht with more than fortune can bestowe,
Goodnesse and Grace, which you doe hold more deere
Than worldly wealth, which melts away like snowe;
Your pleasure is the word of God to heare,
That his most holy precepts you may know:
        Your greatest honour, faire and virtuous deeds,
        Which from the love and feare of God proceeds.

Therefore to you (good Madame) I present
His lovely love, more worth than purest gold,
Who for your sake his pretious blood hath spent,
His death and passion here you may behold,
And view this Lambe, that to the world was sent,
Whom your faire soule may in her armes infold:
        Loving his love, that did endure such paine,
        That you in heaven a worthy place might gaine.

For

For well you knowe, this world is but a Stage
Where all doe play their parts, and must be gone;
Here's no respect of persons, youth, nor age,
Death seizeth all, he never spareth one,
None can prevent or stay that tyrants rage,
But Jesus Christ the Just: By him alone
    He was orecome, He open set the dore
    To Eternall life, ne're seene, nor knowne before.

He is the stone the builders did refuse,
Which you, sweet Lady, are to build upon;
He is the rocke that holy Church did chuse,
Among which number, you must needs be one;
Faire Shepheardesse, 'tis you that he will use
To feed his flocke, that trust in him alone:
    All worldly blessings he vouchsafes to you,
    That to the poore you may returne his due.

And if deserts a Ladies love may gaine,
Then tell me, who hath more deserv'd than he?
Therefore in recompence of all his paine,
Bestowe your paines to reade, and pardon me,
If out of wants, or weakenesse of my braine,
I have not done this worke sufficiently;
    Yet lodge him in the closet of your heart,
    Whose worth is more than can be shew'd by Art.

To

To the Vertuous Reader

OFTEN HAVE I heard, that it is the property of some women, not only to emulate the virtues and perfections
of the rest, but also by all their powers of ill speaking,
to ecclipse the brightnes of their deserved fame: now
contrary to their custome, which men I hope unjustly lay to
their charge, I have written this small volume, or little booke,
for the generall use of all virtuous Ladies and Gentlewomen
of this kingdome; and in commendation of some particular
persons of our owne sexe, such as for the most part, are so well
knowne to my selfe, and others, that I dare undertake Fame
dares not to call any better. And this have I done, to make
knowne to the world, that all women deserve not to be blamed
though some forgetting they are women themselves, and in
danger to be condemned by the wordes of their owne mouthes,
fall into so great an errour, as to speak unadvisedly against
the rest of their sexe; which if it be true, I am perswaded they
can shew their own imperfection in nothing more: and therefore could wish (for their owne ease, modesties, and credit) they
would referre such points of folly, to be practised by evill disposed men, who forgetting they were borne of women, nourished
of women, and that if it were not by the meanes of women, they
would be quite extinguished out of the world, and a finall ende
of them all, doe like Vipers deface the wombes wherein they
were bred, onely to give way and utterance to their want of
discretion and goodnesse. Such as these, were they that disho-
noured Christ his Apostles and Prophets, putting them to
shamefull deaths. Therefore we are not to regard any imputations, that they undeservedly lay upon us, no otherwise than
to make use of them to our owne benefits, as spurres to ver-
tue, making us flie all occasions that may colour their unjust

speeches

speeches to passe currant. Especially considering that they have
tempted even the patience of God himselfe, who gave power to
wise and virtuous women, to bring down their pride and ar-
rogancie. As was cruell *Cesarus* by the discreet counsell of noble *Deborah*, Judge and Prophetesse of Israel : and resolution
of *Jael* wife of *Heber* the Kenite : wicked *Haman*, by the divine prayers and prudent proceedings of beautiful *Hester* :
blasphemous *Holofernes*, by the invincible courage, rare wisdome, and confident carriage of *Judeth* : and the unjust Judges,
by the innocency of chast *Susanna* : with infinite others, which
for brevitie sake I will omit. As also in respect it pleased our
Lord and Saviour Jesus Christ, without the assistance of man,
beeing free from originall and all other sinnes, from the time
of his conception, till the houre of his death, to be begotten of a
woman, borne of a woman, nourished of a woman, obedient to a
woman ; and that he healed women, pardoned women, comforted women : yea, even when he was in his greatest agonie and
bloodie sweat, going to be crucified, and also in the last houre
of his death, tooke care to dispose of a woman : after his resurrection, appeared first to a woman, sent a woman to declare his
most glorious resurrection to the rest of his Disciples. Many
other examples I could alleadge of divers faithfull and virtuous women, who have in all ages, not onely beene Confessors,
but also indured most cruel martyrdome for their faith in Jesus Christ. All which is sufficient to inforce all good Christians and honourable minded men to speak reverently of our
sexe, and especially of all virtuous and good women. To the
modest sensures of both which, I refer these my imperfect in-
deavours, knowing that according to their owne excellent di-
spositions, they will rather, cherish, nourish, and increase the
least sparke of virtue where they find it, by their favourable
and best interpretations, than quench it by wrong constructions. To whom I wish all increase of virtue, and desire their
best opinions.

Salve Deus Rex Judæorum

Sith *Cynthia* is ascended to that rest
  Of endlesse joy and true Eternitie,
  That glorious place that cannot be exprest
By any wight clad in mortalitie,
In her almightie love so highly blest,
And crown'd with everlasting Sov'raigntie;
    Where Saints and Angells do attend her Throne,
    And she gives glorie unto God alone.

¶ To thee great Countesse now I will applie
My Pen, to write thy never dying fame;
That when to Heav'n thy blessed Soule shall flie,
These lines on earth record thy reverend name:
And to this taske I meane my Muse to tie,
Though wanting skill I shall but purchase blame:
    Pardon (deere Ladie) want of womans wit
    To pen thy praise, when few can equall it.

*The Ladie
Margaret
Countesse
Dowager of
Cumberland*

And pardon (Madame) though I do not write
Those praisefull lines of that delightfull place,
As you commaunded me in that faire night,
When shining *Phoebe* gave so great a grace,
Presenting *Paradice* to your sweet sight,
Unfolding all the beauty of her face
    With pleasant groves, hills, walks and stately trees,
    Which pleasures with retired minds agrees.

Whose

Whose Eagles eyes behold the glorious Sunne
Of th'all-creating Providence, reflecting
His blessed beames on all by him, begunne;
Increasing, strengthning, guiding and directing
All worldly creatures their due course to runne,
Unto His powrefull pleasure all subjecting:
    And thou (deere Ladie) by his speciall grace,
    In these his creatures dost behold his face.

Whose all-reviving beautie, yeelds such joyes
To thy sad Soule, plunged in waves of woe,
That worldly pleasures seemes to thee as toyes,
Onely thou seek'st Eternitie to know,
Respecting not the infinite annoyes
That Satan to thy well-staid mind can show;
    Ne can he quench in thee, the Spirit of Grace,
    Nor draw thee from beholding Heavens bright face.

Thy Mind so perfect by thy Maker fram'd,
No vaine delights can harbour in thy heart,
With his sweet love, thou art so much inflam'd,
As of the world thou seem'st to have no part;
So, love him still, thou need'st not be asham'd,
Tis He that made thee, what thou wert, and art:
    Tis He that dries all teares from Orphans eies,
    And heares from heav'n the wofull widdows cries.

Tis He that doth behold thy inward cares,
And will regard the sorrowes of thy Soule;
Tis He that guides thy feet from Sathans snares,
And in his Wisedome, doth thy waies controule:
He through afflictions, still thy Minde prepares,
And all thy glorious Trialls will enroule:
    That when darke daies of terror shall appeare,
    Thou as the Sunne shalt shine; or much more cleare.

The

The Heavn's shall perish as a garment olde,
Or as a vesture by the maker chang'd,
And shall depart, as when a skrowle is rolde;
Yet thou from him shalt never be estrang'd,
When He shall come in glory, that was solde
For all our sinnes; we happily are chang'd,
    Who for our faults put on his righteousnesse,
    Although full oft his Lawes we doe transgresse.

Long mai'st thou joy in this almightie love,
Long may thy Soule be pleasing in his sight,
Long mai'st thou have true comforts from above,
Long mai'st thou set on him thy whole delight,
And patiently endure when he doth prove,
Knowing that He will surely do thee right:
    Thy patience, faith, long suffring, and thy love,
    He will reward with comforts from above.

With Majestie and Honour is He clad,
And deck'd with light, as with a garment faire;
He joyes the Meeke, and makes the Mightie sad,
Pulls down the Prowd, and doth the Humble reare:
Who sees this Bridegroome, never can be sad;
None lives that can his wondrous workes declare:
    Yea, looke how farre the Est is from the West,
    So farre he sets our sinnes that have transgrest.

He rides upon the wings of all the windes,
And spreads the heav'ns with all powrefull hand;
Oh! who can loose when the Almightie bindes?
Or in his angry presence dares to stand?
He searcheth out the secrets of all mindes;
And those that feare him shall possesse the Land:
    He is exceeding glorious to behold,
    Antient of Times; so faire, and yet so old.

He

He of the watry Cloudes his Chariot frames,
And makes his blessed Angels powrefull Spirits,
His ministers are fearefull fiery flames,
Rewarding all according to their merits;
The Righteous for an heritage he claimes,
And registers the wrongs of humble spirits:
    Hills melt like wax, in presence of the Lord,
    So do all sinners, in his sight abhorr'd.

He in the waters laies his chamber beames,
And cloudes of darkenesse compasse him about,
Consuming fire shall goe before in streames,
And burne up all his en'mies round about:
Yet on these Judgements worldlings never dreames,
Nor of these daungers never stand in doubt:
    While he shall rest within his holy Hill,
    That lives and dies according to his Will.

But woe to them that double-hearted bee,
Who with their tongues the righteous Soules doe slay;
Bending their bowes to shoot at all they see,
With upright hearts their Maker to obay;
And secretly doe let their arrowes flee,
To wound true hearted people any way:
    The Lord wil roote them out that speake prowd things,
    Deceitfull tongues are but false Slanders wings.

Froward are the ungodly from their berth,
No sooner borne, but they doe goe astray;
The Lord will roote them out from off the earth,
And give them to their en'mies for a pray,
As venemous as Serpents is their breath,
With poysoned lies to hurt in what they may
    The Innocent: who as a Dove shall flie
    Unto the Lord, that he his cause may trie.

The

Lucy Harington, Countess of Bedford

Margaret Russell, Countess of Cumberland

The righteous Lord doth righteousnesse allow,
His countenance will behold the thing that's just;
Unto the Meane he makes the Mightie bow,
And raiseth up the Poore out of the dust:
Yet makes no count to us, nor when, nor how,
But powres his grace on all, that puts their trust
    In him: that never will their hopes betray
    Nor lets them perish that for mercie pray.

He shall within his Tabernacle dwell,
Whose life is uncorrupt before the Lord,
Who no untrueths of Innocents doth tell,
Nor wrongs his neighbour, nor in deed, nor word,
Nor in his pride with malice seems to swell,
Nor whets his tongue more sharper than a sword,
    To wound the reputation of the Just;
    Nor seekes to lay their glorie in the Dust.

That great *Jehova* King of heav'n and earth,
Will raine downe fire and brimstone from above,
Upon the wicked monsters in their berth
That storme and rage at those whom he doth love:
Snares, stormes, and tempests he will raine, and dearth,
Because he will himselfe almightie prove:
    And this shall be the portion they shall drinke,
    That thinkes the Lord is blind when he doth winke.

¶ Pardon (good Madame) though I have digrest   *To the Coun-*
From what I doe intend to write of thee,   *tesse of Cum-*
To set his glorie forth whom thou lov'st best,   *berland.*
Whose wondrous works no mortal eie can see;
His speciall care on those whom he hath blest
From wicked worldlings, how he sets them free:
    And how such people he doth overthrow
    In all their waies, that they his powre may know.

G   [83]   The

The meditation of this Monarchs love,
Drawes thee from caring what this world can yield;
Of joyes and griefes both equall thou dost prove,
They have no force, to force thee from the field:
Thy constant faith like to the Turtle Dove
Continues combat, and will never yield
To base affliction, or prowd pomps desire,
That sets the weakest mindes so much on fire.

Thou from the Court to the Countrie art retir'd,
Leaving the world, before the world leaves thee:
That great Enchantresse of weake mindes admir'd,
Whose all-bewitching charmes so pleasing be
To worldly wantons; and too much desir'd
Of those that care not for Eternitie:
But yeeld themselves as preys to Lust and Sinne,
Loosing their hopes of Heav'n Hell paines to winne.

But thou, the wonder of our wanton age
Leav'st all delights to serve a heav'nly King:
Who is more wise? or who can be more sage,
Than she that doth Affection subject bring;
Not forcing for the world, or Satans rage,
But shrowding under the Almighties wing;
Spending her yeares, moneths, daies, minutes, howres,
In doing service to the heav'nly powres.

Thou faire example, live without compare,
With Honours triumphs seated in thy breast;
Pale Envy never can thy name empaire,
When in thy heart thou harbour'st such a guest:
Malice must live for ever in dispaire;
There's no revenge where Virtue still doth rest:
All hearts must needs do homage unto thee,
In whom all eies such rare perfection see.

That

That outward Beautie which the world commends,
Is not the subject I will write upon,
Whose date expir'd, that tyrant Time soone ends;
Those gawdie colours soone are spent and gone:
But those faire Virtues which on thee attends
Are alwaies fresh, they never are but one:
    They make thy Beautie fairer to behold,
    Than was that Queenes for whom prowd *Troy* was sold.

An Invective against outward beuty unaccompanied with virtue.

As for those matchlesse colours Red and White,
Or perfit features in a fading face,
Or due proportion pleasing to the sight;
All those doe draw but dangers and disgrace:
A mind enrich'd with Virtue, shines more bright,
Addes everlasting Beauty, gives true grace,
    Frames an immortall Goddesse on the earth,
    Who though she dies, yet Fame gives her new berth.

That pride of Nature which adornes the faire,
Like blasing Comets to allure all eies,
Is but the thred, that weaves their web of Care,
Who glories most, where most their danger lies;
For greatest perills do attend the faire,
When men do seeke, attempt, plot and devise,
    How they may overthrow the chastest Dame,
    Whose Beautie is the White whereat they aime.

Twas Beautie bred in *Troy* the ten yeares strife,
And carried *Hellen* from her lawfull Lord;
Twas Beautie made chaste *Lucrece* loose her life,
For which prowd *Tarquins* fact was so abhorr'd:
Beautie the cause *Antonius* wrong'd his wife,
Which could not be decided but by sword:
    Great *Cleopatraes* Beautie and defects
    Did worke *Octaviaes* wrongs, and his neglects.

What

What fruit did yeeld that faire forbidden tree,
But blood, dishonour, infamie, and shame?
Poore blinded Queene, could'st thou no better see,
But entertaine disgrace, in stead of fame?
Doe these designes with Majestie agree?
To staine thy blood, and blot thy royall name.
    That heart that gave consent unto this ill,
    Did give consent that thou thy selfe should'st kill.

Of Rosa-   ¶ Faire *Rosamund*, the wonder of her time,
mund   Had bin much fairer, had shee not bin faire;
Beautie betraid her thoughts, aloft to clime,
To build strong castles in uncertaine aire,
Where th'infection of a wanton crime
Did worke her fall; first poyson, then despaire,
    With double death did kill her perjur'd soule,
    When heavenly Justice did her sinne controule.

Of Matilda   ¶ Holy *Matilda* in a haplesse houre
Was borne to sorrow and to discontent,
Beauty the cause that turn'd her Sweet to Soure,
While Chastity fought Folly to prevent.
Lustfull King *John* refus'd, did use his powre,
By Fire and Sword, to compasse his content:
    But Friends disgrace, nor Fathers banishment,
    Nor Death it selfe, could purchase her consent.

Here Beauty in the height of all perfection,
Crown'd this faire Creatures everlasting fame,
Whose noble minde did scorne the base subjection
Of Feares, or Favours, to impaire her Name:
By heavenly grace, she had such true direction,
To die with Honour, not to live in Shame;
    And drinke that poyson with a cheerefull heart,
    That could all Heavenly grace to her impart.

This

¶ This Grace great Lady, doth possesse thy Soule,
And makes thee pleasing in thy Makers sight;
This Grace doth all imperfect Thoughts controule,
Directing thee to serve thy God aright;
Still reckoning him, the Husband of thy Soule,
Which is most pretious in his glorious sight:
    Because the Worlds delights shee doth denie
    For him, who for her sake vouchsaf'd to die.

To the Ladie of Cumber- land the In- troduction to the passion of Christ.

And dying made her Dowager of all;
Nay more, Co-heire of that eternall blisse
That Angels lost, and We by *Adams* fall;
Meere Cast-awaies, rais'd by a *Judas* kisse,
Christs bloody sweat, the Vineger, and Gall,
The Speare, Sponge, Nailes, his buffeting with Fists,
    His bitter Passion, Agony, and Death,
    Did gaine us Heaven when He did loose his breath.

¶ These high deserts invites my lowely Muse
To write of Him, and pardon crave of thee,
For Time so spent, I need make no excuse,
Knowing it doth with thy faire Minde agree
So well, as thou no Labour wilt refuse,
That to thy holy Love may pleasing be:
    His Death and Passion I desire to write,
    And thee to read, the blessed Soules delight.

A preamble of the Au- thor before the Passion.

But my deare Muse, now whither wouldst thou flie,
Above the pitch of thy appointed straine?
With *Icarus* thou seekest now to trie,
Not waxen wings, but thy poore barren Braine,
Which farre too weake, these siely lines descrie;
Yet cannot this thy forward Mind restraine,
    But thy poore Infant Verse must soare aloft,
    Not fearing threat'ning dangers, happening oft.

Thinke

Thinke when the eye of Wisdom shall discover
Thy weakling Muse to flie, that scarce could creepe,
And in the Ayre above the Clowdes to hover,
When better 'twere mued up, and fast asleepe;
They'l thinke with *Phaeton*, thou canst neare recover,
But helplesse with that poore yong Lad to weepe:
    The little World of thy weake Wit on fire,
    Where thou wilt perish in thine owne desire.

But yet the Weaker thou doest seeme to be
In Sexe, or Sence, the more his Glory shines,
That doth infuze such powerfull Grace in thee,
To shew thy Love in these few humble Lines;
The Widowes Myte, with this may well agree,
Her little All more worth than golden mynes,
    Beeing more deerer to our loving Lord,
    Than all the wealth that Kingdoms could afford.

Therefore I humbly for his Grace will pray,
That he will give me Power and Strength to Write,
That what I have begun, so end I may,
As his great Glory may appeare more bright;
Yea in these Lines I may no further stray,
Than his most holy Spirit shall give me Light:
    That blindest Weakenesse be not over-bold,
    The manner of his Passion to unfold.

In other Phrases than may well agree
With his pure Doctrine, and most holy Writ,
That Heavens cleare eye, and all the World may see,
I seeke his Glory, rather than to get
The Vulgars breath, the seed of Vanitie,
Nor Fames lowd Trumpet care I to admit;
    But rather strive in plainest Words to showe,
    The Matter which I seeke to undergoe.

A Mat-

A Matter farre beyond my barren skill,
To shew with any Life this map of Death,
This Storie; that whole Worlds with Bookes would fill,
In these few Lines, will put me out of breath,
To run so swiftly up this mightie Hill,
I may behold it with the eye of Faith;
    But to present this pure unspotted Lambe,
    I must confesse, I farre unworthy am.

Yet if he please t'illuminate my Spirit,
And give me Wisdom from his holy Hill,
That I may Write part of his glorious Merit,
If he vouchsafe to guide my Hand and Quill,
To shew his Death, by which we doe inherit
Those endlesse Joyes that all our hearts doe fill;
    Then will I tell of that sad black fac'd Night,
    Whose mourning Mantle covered Heavenly Light.

¶ That very Night our Saviour was betrayed,   *Here begins*
Oh night! exceeding all the nights of sorow,   *the Passion of*
When our most blessed Lord, although dismayed,   *Christ.*
Yet would not he one Minutes respite borrow,
But to *Mount Olives* went, though sore afraid,
To welcome Night, and entertaine the Morrow;
    And as he oft unto that place did goe,
    So did he now, to meet his long nurst woe.

He told his deere Disciples that they all
Should be offended by him, that selfe night,
His Griefe was great, and theirs could not be small,
To part from him who was their sole Delight;
Saint *Peter* thought his Faith could never fall,
No mote could happen in so cleare a sight:
    Which made him say, though all men were offended,
    Yet would he never, though his life were ended.

          But

But his deare Lord made answere, That before
The Cocke did crowe, he should deny him thrice;
This could not choose but grieve him very sore,
That his hot Love should proove more cold than Ice,
Denying him he did so much adore;
No imperfection in himselfe he spies,
      But faith againe, with him hee'l surely die,
      Rather than his deare Master once denie.

And all the rest (did likewise say the same)
Of his Disciples, at that instant time;
But yet poore *Peter*, he was most too blame,
That thought above them all, by Faith to clime;
His forward speech inflicted sinne and shame,
When Wisdoms eyes did looke and checke his crime:
      Who did foresee, and told it him before,
      Yet would he needs averre it more and more.

Now went our Lord unto that holy place,
Sweet *Gethsemaine* hallowed by his presence,
That blessed Garden, which did now embrace
His holy corps, yet could make no defence
Against those Vipers, objects of disgrace,
Which sought that pure eternall Love to quench:
      Here his Disciples willed he to stay,
      Whilst he went further, where he meant to pray.

None were admitted with their Lord to goe,
But *Peter*, and the sonnes of Zebed'us,
To them good *Jesus* opened all his woe,
He gave them leave his sorows to discusse,
His deepest griefes, he did not scorne to showe
These three deere friends, so much he did intrust:
      Beeing sorowfull, and overcharg'd with griefe,
      He told it them, yet look'd for no reliefe.

Sweet

Sweet Lord, how couldst thou thus to flesh and blood
Communicate thy griefe? tell of thy woes?
Thou knew'st they had no powre to doe thee good,
But were the cause thou must endure these blowes,
Beeing the Scorpions bred in *Adams* mud,
Whose poys'ned sinnes did worke among thy foes,
 To re-ore-charge thy over-burd'ned soule,
 Although the sorowes now they doe condole.

Yet didst thou tell them of thy troubled state,
Of thy Soules heavinesse unto the death,
So full of Love, so free wert thou from hate,
To bid them stay, whose sinnes did stop thy breath,
When thou wert entring at so straite a gate,
Yea entring even into the doore of Death,
 Thou bidst them tarry there, and watch with thee,
 Who from thy pretious blood-shed were not free.

Bidding them tarry, thou didst further goe,
To meet affliction in such gracefull sort,
As might moove pitie both in friend and foe,
Thy sorowes such, as none could them comport,
Such great Indurements who did ever know,
When to th'Almighty thou didst make resort?
 And falling on thy face didst humbly pray,
 If 'twere his Will that Cup might passe away.

Saying, Not my will, but thy will Lord be done.
When as thou prayedst an Angel did appeare
From Heaven, to comfort thee Gods onely Sonne,
That thou thy Suffrings might'st the better beare,
Beeing in an agony, thy glasse neere run,
Thou prayedst more earnestly, in so great feare,
 That pretious sweat came trickling to the ground,
 Like drops of blood thy sences to confound.

Loe

Loe here his Will, not thy Will, Lord was done,
And thou content to undergoe all paines,
Sweet Lambe of God, his deare beloved Sonne,
By this great purchase, what to thee remaines?
Of Heaven and Earth thou hast a Kingdom wonne,
Thy Glory beeing equall with thy Gaines,
    In ratifying Gods promise on the Earth,
    Made many hundred yeares before thy birth.

But now returning to thy sleeping Friends,
That could not watch one houre for love of thee,
Even those three Friends, which on thy Grace depends,
Yet shut those Eies that should their Maker see;
What colour, what excuse, or what amends,
From thy Displeasure now can set them free?
    Yet thy pure Pietie bids them Watch and Pray,
    Lest in Temptation they be led away.

Although the Spirit was willing to obay,
Yet what great weakenesse in the Flesh was found!
They slept in Ease, whilst thou in Paine didst pray;
Loe, they in Sleepe, and thou in Sorow drown'd:
Yet Gods right Hand was unto thee a stay,
When horror, griefe, and sorow did abound:
    His Angel did appeare from Heaven to thee,
    To yeeld thee comfort in Extremitie.

But what could comfort then thy troubled Minde,
When Heaven and Earth were both against thee bent?
And thou no hope, no ease, no rest could'st finde,
But must restore that Life, which was but lent;
Was ever creature in the World so kinde,
But he that from Eternitie was sent?
    To satisfie for many Worlds of Sinne,
    Whose matchless Torments did but then begin.

If

If one Mans sinne doth challendge Death and Hell,
With all the Torments that belong thereto:
If for one sinne such Plagues on *David* fell,
As grieved him, and did his Seed undoe:
If *Salomon*, for that he did not well,
Falling from Grace, did loose his Kingdome too:
    Ten Tribes beeing taken from his wilfull Sonne
    And Sinne the Cause that they were all undone.

What could thy Innocency now expect,
When all the Sinnes that ever were committed,
Were laid to thee, whom no man could detect?
Yet farre thou wert of Man from beeing pittied,
The Judge so just could yeeld thee no respect,
Nor would one jot of penance be remitted;
    But greater horror to thy Soule must rise,
    Than Heart can thinke, or any Wit devise.

Now drawes the houre of thy affliction neere,
And ugly Death presents himselfe before thee;
Thou now must leave those Friends thou held'st so deere,
Yea those Disciples, who did most adore thee;
Yet in thy countenance doth no Wrath appeare,
Although betrayd to those that did abhorre thee:
    Thou did'st vouchsafe to visit them againe,
    Who had no apprehension of thy paine.

Their eyes were heavie, and their hearts asleepe,
Nor knew they well what answere then to make thee;
Yet thou as Watchman, had'st a care to keepe
Those few from sinne, that shortly would forsake thee;
But now thou bidst them henceforth Rest and Sleepe,
Thy houre is come, and they at hand to take thee:
    The sonne of God to Sinners made a pray,
    Oh hatefull houre! oh blest! oh cursed day!

Loe

Loe here thy great Humility was found,
Beeing King of Heaven, and Monarch of the Earth,
Yet well content to have thy Glory drownd,
By beeing counted of so meane a berth;
Grace, Love, and Mercy did so much abound,
Thou entertaindst the Crosse, even to the death:
 And nam'dst thy selfe, the sonne of Man to be,
 To purge our pride by thy Humilitie.

But now thy friends whom thou didst call to goe,
Heavy Spectators of thy haplesse case,
See thy Betrayer, whom too well they knowe,
One of the twelve, now object of disgrace,
A trothlesse traytor, and a mortall foe,
With fained kindnesse seekes thee to imbrace;
 And gives a kisse, whereby he may deceive thee,
 That in the hands of Sinners he might leave thee.

Now muster forth with Swords, with Staves, with Bils,
High Priests and Scribes, and Elders of the Land,
Seeking by force to have their wicked Wils,
Which thou didst never purpose to withstand;
Now thou mak'st haste unto the worst of Ils,
And who they seeke, thou gently doest demand;
 This didst thou Lord, t'amaze these Fooles the more,
 T'inquire of that, thou knew'st so well before.

When loe these Monsters did not shame to tell,
His name they sought, and found, yet could not know
Jesus of Nazareth, at whose feet they fell,
When Heavenly Wisdome did descend so lowe
To speake to them; they knew they did not well,
Their great amazement made them backeward goe:
 Nay, though he said unto them, I am he,
 They could not know him, whom their eyes did see.

How

How blinde were they could not discerne the Light!
How dull! if not to understand the truth,
How weake! if meekenesse overcame their might;
How stony hearted, if not mov'd to ruth:
How void of Pitie, and how full of Spight,
Gainst him that was the Lord of Light and Truth:
    Here insolent Boldnesse checkt by Love and Grace,
    Retires, and falls before our Makers face.

For when he spake to this accursed crew,
And mildely made them know that it was he:
Presents himselfe, that they might take a view;
And what they doubted they might cleerely see;
Nay more, to re-assure that it was true,
He said: I say unto you, I am hee.
    If him they sought, he's willing to obay,
    Onely desires the rest might goe their way.

Thus with a heart prepared to endure
The greatest wrongs Impietie could devise,
He was content to stoope unto their Lure,
Although his Greatnesse might doe otherwise:
Here Grace was seised on with hands impure,
And Virtue now must be supprest by Vice,
    Pure Innocencie made a prey to Sinne,
    Thus did his Torments and our Joyes beginne.

Here faire Obedience shined in his breast,
And did suppresse all feare of future paine;
Love was his Leader unto this unrest,
Whil'st Righteousnesse doth carry up his Traine;
Mercy made way to make us highly blest,
When Patience beat downe Sorrow, Feare and Paine:
    Justice sate looking with an angry brow,
    On blessed misery appeering now.

            More

More glorious than all the Conquerors
That ever liv'd within this Earthly round,
More powrefull than all Kings, or Governours
That ever yet within this World were found;
More valiant than the greatest Souldiers
That ever fought, to have their glory crown'd:
    For which of them, that ever yet tooke breath,
    Sought t'indure the doome of Heaven and Earth?

But our sweet Saviour whom these Jewes did name;
Yet could their learned Ignorance apprehend
No light of grace, to free themselves from blame:
Zeale, Lawes, Religion, now they doe pretend
Against the truth, untruths they seeke to frame:
Now al their powres, their wits, their strengths, they bend
    Against one siely, weake, unarmed man,
    Who no resistance makes, though much he can,

To free himselfe from these unlearned men,
Who call'd him Saviour in his blessed name;
Yet farre from knowing him their Saviour then,
That came to save both them and theirs from blame;
Though they retire and fall, they come agen
To make a surer purchase of their shame:
    With lights and torches now they find the way,
    To take the Shepheard whilst the sheep doe stray.

Why should unlawfull actions use the Light?
Inniquitie in Darkenesse seekes to dwell;
Sinne rides his circuit in the dead of Night,
Teaching all soules the ready waies to hell;
Sathan coms arm'd with all the powres of Spight,
Heartens his Champions, makes them rude and fell;
    Like rav'ning wolves, to shed his guiltlesse blood,
    Who thought no harme, but di'd to doe them good.

Here

Here Falshood beares the shew of formall Right,
Base Treacherie hath gote a guard of men;
Tyranny attends, with all his strength and might,
To leade this siely Lamb to Lyons denne;
Yet he unmoov'd in this most wretched plight,
Goes on to meete them, knowes the houre, and when:
    The powre of darkenesse must expresse Gods ire,
    Therefore to save these few was his desire.

These few that wait on Poverty and Shame,
And offer to be sharers in his Ils;
These few that will be spreaders of his Fame,
He will not leave to Tyrants wicked wils;
But still desires to free them from all blame,
Yet Feare goes forward, Anger Patience kils:
    A Saint is mooved to revenge a wrong,
    And Mildnesse doth what doth to Wrath belong.

For *Peter* griev'd at what might then befall,
Yet knew not what to doe, nor what to thinke,
Thought something must be done; now, if at all,
To free his Master, that he might not drinke
This poys'ned draught, farre bitterer than gall,
For now he sees him at the very brinke
    Of griesly Death, who gins to shew his face,
    Clad in all colours of a deepe disgrace.

And now those hands that never us'd to fight,
Or drawe a weapon in his owne defence,
Too forward is, to doe his Master right,
Since of his wrongs, hee feeles so true a sence:
But ah poore *Peter*! now thou wantest might,
And hee's resolv'd, with them he will goe hence:
    To draw thy sword in such a helpelesse cause,
    Offends thy Lord, and is against the Lawes.

So

So much he hates Revenge, so farre from Hate,
That he vouchsafes to heale, whom thou dost wound;
His paths are Peace, with none he holdes Debate,
His Patience stands upon so sure a ground,
To counsell thee, although it comes too late:
Nay, to his foes, his mercies so abound,
 That he in pitty doth thy will restraine,
 And heales the hurt, and takes away the paine.

For willingly he will endure this wrong,
Although his pray'rs might have obtain'd such grace,
As to dissolve their plots though ne'r so strong,
And bring these wicked Actors in worse case
Than *Ægypts* King on whom Gods plagues did throng,
But that foregoing Scriptures must take place:
 If God by prayers had an army sent
 Of powrefull Angels, who could them prevent?

Yet mightie JESUS meekely ask'd, Why they
With Swords and Staves doe come as to a Thiefe?
Hee teaching in the Temple day by day
None did offend, or give him cause of griefe.
Now all are forward, glad is he that may
Give most offence, and yeeld him least reliefe:
 His hatefull foes are ready now to take him,
 And all his deere Disciples do forsake him.

Those deare Disciples that he most did love,
And were attendant at his becke and call,
When triall of affliction came to prove,
They first left him, who now must leave them all:
For they were earth, and he came from above,
Which made them apt to flie, and fit to fall:
 Though they protest they never will forsake him,
 They do like men, when dangers overtake them.

And

Katherine Knevet, Countess of Suffolk

Anne Clifford, Countess of Dorset

And he alone is bound to loose us all,
Whom with unhallowed hands they led along,
To wicked *Caiphas* in the Judgement Hall,
Who studies onely how to doe him wrong;
High Priests and Elders, People great and small,
With all reprochfull words about him throng:
    False Witnesses are now call'd in apace,
    Whose trothelesse tongues must make pale death imbrace

The beauty of the World, Heavens chiefest Glory;
The mirrour of Martyrs, Crowne of holy Saints;
Love of th'Almighty, blessed Angels story;
Water of Life, which none that drinks it, faints;
Guide of the Just, where all our Light we borrow;
Mercy of Mercies; Hearer of Complaints;
    Triumpher over Death; Ransomer of Sinne;
    Falsely accused: now his paines begin.

Their tongues doe serve him as a Passing bell,
For what they say is certainly beleeved;
So sound a tale unto the Judge they tell,
That he of Life must shortly be bereaved;
Their share of Heaven, they doe not care to sell,
So his afflicted Heart be throughly grieved:
    They tell his Words, though farre from his intent,
    And what his Speeches were, not what he meant.

That he Gods holy Temple could destroy,
And in three daies could build it up againe;
This seem'd to them a vaine and idle toy,
It would not sinke into their sinful braine:
Christs blessed body, al true Christians joy,
Should die, and in three dayes revive againe:
    This did the Lord of Heaven and earth endure,
    Unjustly to be charg'd by tongues impure.

And now they all doe give attentive care,
To heare the answere, which he will not make;
The people wonder how he can forbeare,
And these great wrongs so patiently can take;
But yet he answers not, nor doth he care,
Much more he will endure for our sake:
    Nor can their wisdoms any way discover,
    Who he should be that proov'd so true a Lover.

To entertaine the sharpest pangs of death,
And fight a combate in the depth of hell,
For wretched Worldlings made of dust and earth,
Whose harden'd hearts, with pride and mallice swell;
In midst of bloody sweat, and dying breath,
He had compassion on these tyrants fell:
    And purchast them a place in Heav'n forever,
    When they his Soule and Body sought to sever.

Sinnes ugly mists, so blinded had their eyes,
That at Noone dayes they could discerne no Light;
These were those fooles, that thought themselves so wise,
The Jewish wolves, that did our Saviour bite;
For now they use all meanes they can devise,
To beate downe truth, and goe against all right:
    Yea now they take Gods holy name in vaine,
    To know the truth, which truth they doe prophane.

The chiefest Hel-hounds of this hatefull crew,
Rose up to aske what answere he could make,
Against those false accusers in his view;
That by his speech, they might advantage take:
He held his peace, yet knew they said not true,
No answere would his holy wisdome make,
    Till he was charged in his glorious name,
    Whose pleasure 'twas he should endure this shame.

Then

Then with so mild a Majestie he spake,
As they might easly know from whence he came,
His harmelesse tongue doth no exceptions take,
Nor Priests, nor People, meanes he now to blame;
But answers Folly, for true Wisdomes sake,
Beeing charged deeply by his powrefull name,
    To tell if Christ the Sonne of God he be,
    Who for our sinnes must die, to set us free.

To thee O *Caiphas* doth he answere give,
That thou hast said, what thou desir'st to know,
And yet thy malice will not let him live,
So much thou art unto thy selfe a foe;
He speaketh truth, but thou wilt not beleeve,
Nor canst thou apprehend it to be so:
    Though he expresse his Glory unto thee,
    Thy Owly eies are blind, and cannot see.

Thou rend'st thy cloathes, in stead of thy false heart,
And on the guiltlesse lai'st thy guilty crime;
For thou blasphem'st, and he must feele the smart:
To sentence death, thou think'st it now high time;
No witnesse now thou need'st, for this fowle part,
Thou to the height of wickednesse canst clime:
    And give occasion to the ruder sort,
    To make afflictions, sorrows, follies sport.

Now when the dawne of day gins to appeare,
And all your wicked counsels have an end,
To end his Life, that holds you all so deere,
For to that purpose did your studies bend;
Proud *Pontius Pilate* must the matter heare,
To your untroths, his eares he now must lend:
    Sweet *Jesus* bound, to him you led away,
    Of his most pretious blood to make your pray.

Which,

Which, when that wicked Caytife did perceive,
By whose lewd meanes he came to this distresse;
He brought the price of blood he did receive,
Thinking thereby to make his fault seeme lesse,
And with these Priests and Elders did it leave,
Confest his fault, wherein he did transgresse:
  But when he saw Repentance unrespected,
  He hang'd himselfe; of God and Man rejected.

By this Example, what can be expected
From wicked Man, which on the Earth doth live?
But faithlesse dealing, feare of God neglected;
Who for their private gaine cares not to sell
The Innocent Blood of Gods most deere elected,
As did that caytife wretch, now damn'd in Hell:
  If in Christs Schoole, he tooke so great a fall,
  What will they doe, that come not there at all.

Now *Pontius Pilate* is to judge the Cause
Of faultlesse *Jesus*, who before him stands;
Who neither hath offended Prince, nor Lawes,
Although he now be brought in woefull bands:
O noble Governour, make thou yet a pause,
Doe not in innocent blood imbrue thy hands;
  But heare the words of thy most worthy wife,
  Who sends to thee, to beg her Saviours life.

Let barb'rous crueltie farre depart from thee,
And in true Justice take afflictions part;
Open thine eies, that thou the truth mai'st see,
Doe not the thing that goes against thy heart,
Condemne not him that must thy Saviour be;
But view his holy Life, his good desert.
  Let not us Women glory in Mens fall,
  Who had power given to over-rule us all.

Till

¶ Till now your indiscretion sets us free
And makes our former fault much less appeare;
Our Mother *Eve*, who tasted of the Tree,
Giving to *Adam* what shee held most deare,
Was simply good, and had no powre to see,
The after-comming harme did not appeare:
> The subtile Serpent that our Sex betraide,
> Before our fall so sure a plot had laide.

That undiscerning Ignorance perceav'd
No guile, or craft that was by him intended;
For had she knowne, of what we were bereav'd,
To his request she had not condiscended.
But she (poor soule) by cunning was deceav'd,
No hurt therein her harmelesse Heart intended:
> For she alleadg'd Gods word, which he denies,
> That they should die, but even as Gods, be wise.

But surely *Adam* can not be excusde,
Her fault though great, yet hee was most too blame;
What Weaknesse offered, Strength might have refusde,
Being Lord of all, the greater was his shame:
Although the Serpents craft had her abusde,
Gods holy word ought all his actions frame,
> For he was Lord and King of all the earth,
> Before poore *Eve* had either life or breath.

Who being fram'd by Gods eternall hand,
The perfect'st man that ever breath'd on earth;
And from Gods mouth receiv'd that strait command,
The breach whereof he knew was present death:
Yea having powre to rule both Sea and Land,
Yet with one Apple wonne to loose that breath
> Which God had breathed in his beauteous face,
> Bringing us all in danger and disgrace.

[103]   And

And then to lay the fault on Patience backe,
That we (poore women) must endure it all;
We know right well he did discretion lacke,
Beeing not perswaded thereunto at all;
If *Eve* did erre, it was for knowledge sake,
The fruit being faire perswaded him to fall:
    No subtill Serpents falshood did betray him,
    If he would eate it, who had powre to stay him?

Not *Eve*, whose fault was onely too much love,
Which made her give this present to her Deare,
That what shee tasted, he likewise might prove,
Whereby his knowledge might become more cleare;
He never sought her weakenesse to reprove,
With those sharpe words, which he of God did heare:
    Yet Men will boast of Knowledge, which he tooke
    From *Eves* faire hand, as from a learned Booke.

If any Evill did in her remaine,
Beeing made of him, he was the ground of all;
If one of many Worlds could lay a staine
Upon our Sexe, and worke so great a fall
To wretched Man, by Satans subtill traine;
What will so fowle a fault amongst you all?
    Her weakenesse did the Serpents words obay,
    But you in malice Gods deare Sonne betray.

Whom, if unjustly you condemne to die,
Her sinne was small, to what you doe commit;
All mortal sinnes that doe for vengeance crie,
Are not to be compared unto it:
If many worlds would altogether trie,
By all their sinnes the wrath of God to get;
    This sinne of yours, surmounts them all as farre
    As doth the Sunne, another little starre.

Then

Then let us have our Libertie againe,
And challendge to your selves no Sov'raigntie;
You came not in the world without our paine,
Make that a barre against your crueltie;
Your fault being greater, why should you disdaine
Our beeing your equals, free from tyranny?
    If one weake woman simply did offend,
    This sinne of yours, hath no excuse, nor end.

To which (poore soules) we never gave consent,
Witnesse thy wife (O *Pilate*) speakes for all;
Who did but dreame, and yet a message sent,
That thou should'st have nothing to doe at all
With that just man; which, if thy heart relent,
Why wilt thou be a reprobate with *Saul*?
    To seeke the death of him that is so good,
    For thy soules health to shed his dearest blood.

Yea, so thou mai'st these sinful people please,
Thou art content against all truth and right,
To seale this act, that may procure thine ease
With blood, and wrong, with tyrannie, and might;
The multitude thou seekest to appease,
By base dejection of this heavenly Light:
    Demanding which of these that thou should'st loose,
    Whether the Thiefe, or Christ King of the Jewes.

Base *Barrabas* the Thiefe, they all desire,
And thou more base than he, perform'st their will;
Yet when thy thoughts backe to themselves retire,
Thou art unwilling to commit this ill:
Oh that thou couldst unto such grace aspire,
That thy polluted lips might never kill
    That Honour, which right Judgement ever graceth,
    To purchase shame, which all true worth defaceth.

Art

Art thou a Judge, and asketh what to do
With one, in whom no fault there can be found?
The death of Christ wilt thou consent unto,
Finding no cause, no reason, nor no ground?
Shall he be scourg'd, and crucified too?
And must his miseries by thy meanes abound?
     Yet not asham'd to aske what he hath done,
     When thine owne conscience seeks this sinne to shunne.

Three times thou ask'st, What evill hath he done?
And saist, thou find'st in him no cause of death,
Yet wilt thou chasten Gods beloved Sonne,
Although to thee no word of ill he saith:
For Wrath must end, what Malice hath begunne,
And thou must yield to stop his guiltlesse breath.
     This rude tumultuous rowt doth presse so sore,
     That thou condemnest him thou shouldst adore.

Yet *Pilate*, this can yeeld thee no content,
To exercise thine owne authoritie,
But unto *Herod* he must needes be sent,
To reconcile thy selfe by tyrannie:
Was this the greatest good in Justice meant,
When thou perceiv'st no fault in him to be?
     If thou must make thy peace by Virtues fall,
     Much better 'twere not to be friends at all.

Yet neither thy sterne browe, nor his great place,
Can draw an answer from the Holy One:
His false accusers, nor his great disgrace,
Nor *Herods* scoffes; to him they are all one:
He neither cares, nor feares his own ill case,
Though being despis'd and mockt of every one:
     King *Herods* gladnesse gives him little ease,
     Neither his anger seekes he to appease.

Yet

Yet this is strange, that base Impietie
Should yeeld those robes of honour, which were due;
Pure white, to shew his great Integritie,
His innocency, that all the world might view;
Perfections height in lowest penury,
Such glorious poverty as they never knew:
    Purple and Scarlet well might him beseeme,
    Whose pretious blood must all the world redeeme.

And that Imperiall Crowne of Thornes he wore,
Was much more pretious than the Diadem
Of any King that ever liv'd before,
Or since his time, their honour's but a dreame
To his eternall glory, beeing so poore,
To make a purchasse of that heavenly Realme;
    Where God with all his Angels lives in peace,
    No griefes, nor sorrowes, but all joyes increase.

Those royall robes, which they in scorne did give,
To make him odious to the common sort,
Yeeld light of Grace to those whose soules shall live
Within the harbour of this heavenly port;
Much doe they joy, and much more doe they grieve,
His death, their life, should make his foes such sport:
    With sharpest thornes to pricke his blessed face,
    Our joyfull sorrow, and his greater grace.

Three feares at once possessed *Pilates* heart;
The first, Christs innocence, which so plaine appeares;
The next, That he which now must feele this smart,
Is Gods deare Sonne, for any thing he heares:
But that which proov'd the deepest wounding dart,
Is Peoples threat'nings, which he so much feares,
    That he to *Caesar* could not be a friend,
    Unlesse he sent sweet JESUS to his end.

Now

Now *Pilate* thou art proov'd a painted wall,
A golden Sepulcher with rotten bones;
From right to wrong, from equitie to fall:
If none upbraid thee, yet the very stones
Will rise against thee, and in question call
His blood, his teares, his sighes, his bitter groanes:
   All these will witnesse at the latter day,
   When water cannot wash thy sinne away.

Canst thou be innocent, that gainst all right,
Wilt yeeld to what thy conscience doth withstand?
Beeing a man of knowledge, powre, and might,
To let the wicked carrie such a hand,
Before thy face to blindfold Heav'ns bright light,
And thou to yeeld to what they did demand?
   Washing thy hands, thy conscience cannot cleare,
   But to all worlds this staine must needs appeare.

For loe, the Guiltie doth accuse the Just,
And faultie Judge condemnes the Innocent;
And wilfull Jewes to exercise their lust,
With whips and taunts against their Lord are bent;
He basely us'd, blasphemed, scorn'd, and curst,
Our heavenly King to death for us they sent:
   Reproches, slanders, spittings in his face,
   Spight doing all her worst in his disgrace.

*Christ going
to death*

¶ And now this long expected houre drawes neere,
When blessed Saints with Angels doe condole;
His holy march, soft pace, and heavy cheere,
In humble sort to yeeld his glorious soule,
By his deserts the fowlest sinnes to cleare;
And in th'eternall booke of heaven to enroule
   A satisfaction till the generall doome,
   Of all sinnes past, and all that are to come.

They

They that had seene this pitifull Procession,
From *Pilates* Palace to Mount Calvarie,
Might thinke he answer'd for some great transgression,
Beeing in such odious sort condemn'd to die;
He plainely shewed that his own profession
Was virtue, patience, grace, love, piety;
    And how by suffering he could conquer more
    Than all the Kings that ever liv'd before.

First went the Crier with open mouth proclayming
The heavy sentence of Iniquitie,
The Hangman next, by his base office clayming
His right in Hell, where sinners never die,
Carrying the nayles, the people still blaspheming
Their maker, using all impiety;
    The Thieves attending him on either side,
    ¶ The Serjeants watching, while the women cri'd.

The teares of the daugh-ters of Jeru-salem.

Thrice happy women that obtained such grace
From him whose worth the world could not containe;
Immediately to turne about his face,
As not remembering his great griefe and paine,
To comfort you, whose teares powr'd forth apace
On *Flora's* bankes, like shewers of Aprils raine:
    Your cries inforced mercie, grace, and love
    From him, whom greatest Princes could not moove

To speake on word, nor once to lift his eyes
Unto proud *Pilate*, no nor *Herod*, king,
By all the Questions that they could devise,
Could make him answere to no manner of thing;
Yet these poore women, by their pitious cries
Bid moove their Lord, their Lover, and their King,
    To take compassion, turne about, and speake
    To them whose hearts were ready now to breake.

Most

Most blessed daughters of Jerusalem,
Who found such favour in your Saviors sight,
To turne his face when you did pitie him;
Your tearefull eyes, beheld his eies more bright;
Your Faith and Love unto such grace did clime,
To have reflection from this Heav'nly Light:
    Your Eagles eyes did gaze against this Sunne,
    Your hearts did thinke, he dead, the world were done.

When spightfull men with torments did oppresse
Th' afflicted body of this innocent Dove,
Poore women seeing how much they did transgresse,
By teares, by sighes, by cries intreat, nay prove,
What may be done among the thickest presse,
They labour still these tyrants hearts to move;
    In pitie and compassion to forbeare
    Their whipping, spurning, tearing of his haire.

But all in vaine, their malice hath no end,
Their hearts more hard than flint, or marble stone;
Now to his griefe, his greatnesse they attend,
When he (God knowes) had rather be alone;
They are his guard, yet seeke all meanes to offend:
Well may he grieve, well may he sigh and groane,
    Under the burthen of a heavy crosse,
    He faintly goes to make their gaine his losse.

The sorrow ¶ His woefull Mother wayting on her Sonne,
of the virgin All comfortlesse in depth of sorow drowned;
Marie. Her griefes extreame, although but new begun,
To see his bleeding body oft she swouned;
How could she choose but thinke her selfe undone,
He dying, with whose glory shee was crowned?
    None ever lost so great a losse as shee,
    Beeing Sonne, and Father of Eternitie.

Her

Her teares did wash away his pretious blood,
That sinners might not tread it under feet
To worship him, and that it did her good
Upon her knees, although in open street,
Knowing he was the Jessie floure and bud,
That must be gather'd when it smell'd most sweet:
 Her Sonne, her Husband, Father, Saviour, King,
 Whose death killd Death, and tooke away his sting.

Most blessed Virgin, in whose faultlesse fruit,
All Nations of the earth must needes rejoyce,
No Creature having sence though ne'r so brute,
But joyes and trembles when they heare his voyce;
His wisedome strikes the wisest persons mute,
Faire chosen vessell, happy in his choyce:
 Deere Mother of our Lord, whose reverend name,
 All people Blessed call, and spread thy fame.

For the Almightie magnified thee,
And looked downe upon thy meane estate;
Thy lowly mind, and unstain'd Chastitie,
Did pleade for Love at great *Jehovaes* gate,
Who sending swift-wing'd *Gabriel* unto thee,
His holy will and pleasure to relate;
 To thee most beauteous Queene of Woman-kind,
 The Angell did unfold his Makers mind.

¶ He thus beganne, Haile *Mary* full of grace,
Thou freely art beloved of the Lord,
He is with thee, behold thy happy case;
What endlesse comfort did these words afford
To thee that saw'st an Angell in the place
Proclaime thy Virtues worth, and to record
 Thee blessed among women: that thy praise
 Should last so many worlds beyond thy daies.

The saluta-
tion of the
virgin Ma-
rie.

[111]

Loe

Loe, this high message to thy troubled spirit,
He doth deliver in the plainest sence;
Sayes, Thou shouldst beare a Sonne that shal inherit
His Father *Davids* throne, free from offence,
Call's him that Holy thing, by whose pure merit
We must be sav'd, tels what he is, of whence;
    His worth, his greatnesse, what his name must be,
    Who should be call'd the Sonne of the most High.

He cheeres thy troubled Soule, bids thee not feare;
When thy pure thoughts could hardly apprehend
This salutation, when he did appeare;
Nor couldst thou judge, whereto those words did tend;
His pure aspect did moove thy modest cheere
To muse, yet joy that God vouchsaf'd to send
    His glorious Angel; who did thee assure
    To beare a child, although a Virgin pure.

Nay more, thy Sonne should Rule and Raigne for ever;
Yea, of his Kingdom there should be no end;
Over the house of *Jacob*, Heavens great Giver
Would give him powre, and to that end did send
His faithfull servant *Gabriel* to deliver
To thy chast eares no word that might offend:
    But that this blessed Infant borne of thee,
    Thy Sonne, The onely Sonne of God should be.

When on the knees of thy submissive heart
Thou humbly didst demand, How that should be?
Thy virgin thoughts did thinke, none could impart
This great good hap, and blessing unto thee;
Farre from desire of any man thou art,
Knowing not one, thou art from all men free:
    When he, to answere this thy chaste desire,
    Gives thee more cause to wonder and admire.

That

That thou a blessed Virgin shouldst remaine,
Yea that the Holy Ghost should come on thee
A maiden Mother, subject to no paine,
For highest powre should overshadow thee:
Could thy faire eyes from teares of joy refraine,
When God look'd downe upon thy poore degree?
    Making thee Servant, Mother, Wife, and Nurse
    To Heavens bright King, that freed us from the curse.

Thus beeing crown'd with glory from above,
Grace and Perfection resting in thy breast,
Thy humble answer doth approove thy Love,
And all these sayings in thy heart doe rest:
Thy Child a Lambe, and thou a Turtle dove,
Above all other women highly blest;
    To find such favour in his glorious sight,
    In whom thy heart and soule doe most delight.

What wonder in the world more strange could seeme,
Than that a Virgin could conceive and beare
Within her wombe a Sonne, That should redeeme
All Nations on the earth, and should repaire
Our old decaies: who in such high esteeme,
Should prize all mortals, living in his feare·
    As not to shun Death, Povertie, and Shame,
    To save their soules, and spread his glorious Name.

And partly to fulfil his Fathers pleasure,
Whose powrefull hand allowes it not for strange,
If he vouchsafe the riches of his treasure,
Pure Righteousnesse to take such il exchange;
On all Iniquitie to make a seisure,
Giving his snow-white Weed for ours in change;
    Our mortall garment in a skarlet Die,
    Too base a roabe for Immortalitie.

Most

Most happy news, that ever yet was brought,
When Poverty and Riches met together,
The wealth of Heaven, in our fraile clothing wrought
Salvation by his happy comming hither:
Mighty Messias, who so deerely bought
Us Slaves to sinne, farre lighter than a feather:
    Toss'd to and fro with every wicked wind,
    The world, the flesh, or Devill gives to blind.

Who on his shoulders our blacke sinnes doth beare
To that most blessed, yet accursed Crosse;
Where fastning them, he rids us of our feare,
Yea for our gaine he is content with losse,
Our ragged clothing scornes he not to weare,
Though foule, rent, torne, disgracefull, rough and grosse,
    Spunne by that monster Sinne, and weav'd by Shame,
    Which grace it selfe, disgrac'd with impure blame.

How canst thou choose (faire Virgin) then but mourne,
When this sweet of-spring of thy body dies,
When thy faire eies beholds his bodie torne,
The peoples fury, heares the womens cries;
His holy name prophan'd, He made a scorne,
Abusde with all their hatefull slaunderous lies:
    Bleeding and fainting in such wondrous sort,
    As scarce his feeble limbes can him support.

Now *Simon* of *Cyrene* passeth them by,
Whom they compell sweet JESUS Crosse to beare
To Golgatha, there doe they meane to trie
All cruell meanes to worke in him dispaire:
That odious place, where dead mens skulls did lie,
There must our Lord for present death prepare:
    His sacred blood must grace that loathsome field,
    To purge more filth, than that foule place could yield.

For

❡ For now arriv'd unto this hatefull place,   *Christs*
In which his Crosse erected needes must bee,   *death.*
False hearts, and willing hands come on apace,
All prest to ill, and all desire to see:
Graceless themselves, still seeking to disgrace;
Bidding him, If the Sonne of God he bee,
  To save himselfe, if he could others save,
  With all th'opprobrious words that might deprave.

His harmelesse hands unto the Crosse they nailde,
And feet that never trode in sinners trace,
Betweene two theeves, unpitied, unbewailde,
Save of some few possessors of his grace,
With sharpest pangs and terrors thus appailde,
Sterne Death makes way, that Life might give him place:
  His eyes with teares, his body full of wounds,
  Death last of paines his sorrows all confounds.

His joynts dis-joynted, and his legges hang downe,
His alablaster breast, his bloody side,
His members torne, and on his head a Crowne
Of sharpest Thorns, to satisfie for pride:
Anguish and Paine doe all his Sences drowne,
While they his holy garments do divide:
  His bowells drie, his heart full fraught with griefe,
  Crying to him that yeelds him no reliefe.

❡ This with the eie of Faith thou maist behold, *To my Ladie*
Deere Spouse of Christ, and more than I can write; *of Cumber-*
And here both Griefe and Joy thou maist unfold, *land.*
To view thy Love in this most heavy plight,
Bowing his head, his bloodlesse body cold;
Those eies waxe dimme that gave us all our light,
  His count'nance pale, yet still continues sweet,
  His blessed blood watring his pierced feet.

O glorious miracle without compare!
Last, but not least which was by him effected;
Uniting death, life, misery, joy and care,
By his sharpe passion in his deere elected:
Who doth the Badges of like Liveries weare,
Shall find how deere they are of him respected.
　　No joy, griefe, paine, life, death, was like to his,
　　Whose infinite dolours wrought eternall blisse.

The terror of　¶ What creature on the earth did then remaine,
all creatures　On whom the horror of this shamefull deed
at that in-　Did not inflict some violent touch, or straine,
stant when　To see the Lord of all the world to bleed?
Christ died.　His dying breath did rend huge rockes in twaine,
　　The heavens betooke them to their mourning weed:
　　　The Sunne grew darke, and scorn'd to give them light,
　　　Who durst ecclipse a glory farre more bright.

The Moone and Starres did hide themselves for shame,
The earth did tremble in her loyall feare,
The Temple vaile did rent to spread his fame,
The Monuments did open every where;
Dead Saints did rise forth of their grave, and came
To divers people that remained there
　　　Within that holy City; whose offence,
　　　Did put their Maker to this large expence.

Things reasonable, and reasonlesse possest
The terrible impression of this fact;
For his oppression made them all opprest,
When with his blood he seal'd so faire an act,
In restlesse miserie to procure our rest;
His glorious deedes that dreadfull prison sackt:
　　　When Death, Hell, Divells, using all their powre,
　　　Were overcome in that most blessed houre.

　　　　　　　Being

Being dead, he killed Death, and did survive
That prowd insulting Tyrant: in whose place
He sends bright Immortalitie to revive
Those whom his yron armes did long embrace;
Who from their loathsome graves brings them alive
In glory to behold their Saviours face:
    Who tooke the keys of all Deaths powre away,
    Opening to those that would his name obay.

O wonder, more than man can comprehend,
Our Joy and Griefe both at one instant fram'd,
Compounded: Contrarieties contend
Each to exceed, yet neither to be blam'd.
Our Griefe to see our Saviours wretched end,
Our Joy to know both Death and Hell he tam'd:
    That we may say, O Death, where is thy sting?
    Hell, yeeld thy victory to thy conq'ring King.

Can stony hearts refraine from shedding teares,
To view the life and death of this sweet Saint?
His austere course in yong and tender yeares,
When great indurements could not make him faint:
His wants, his paines, his torments, and his feares,
All which he undertooke without constraint,
    To shew that infinite Goodnesse must restore,
    What infinite Justice looked for, and more.

Yet, had he beene but of a meane degree,
His suffrings had been small to what they were;
Meane minds will shew of what meane mouldes they bee;
Small griefes seeme great, yet Use doth make them beare:
But ah! tis hard to stirre a sturdy tree;
Great dangers hardly puts great minds in feare:
    They will conceale their griefes which mightie grow
    In their stout hearts untill they overthrow.

If

If then an earthly Prince may ill endure
The least of those afflictions which he bare,
How could this all-commaunding King procure
Such grievous torments with his mind to square,
Legions of Angells being at his Lure?
He might have liv'd in pleasure without care:
    None can conceive the bitter paines he felt,
    When God and Man must suffer without guilt.

Take all the Suffrings Thoughts can thinke upon,
In ev'ry man that this huge world hath bred;
Let all those Paines and Suffrings meet in one,
Yet are they not a Mite to that he did
Endure for us: Oh let us thinke thereon,
That God should have his pretious blood so shed:
    His Greatnesse clothed in our fraile attire,
    And pay so deare a ransom for the hire.

Loe, here was glorie, miserie, life and death,
An union of contraries did accord;
Gladnesse and sadnesse here had one berth,
This wonder wrought the Passion of our Lord,
He suffring for all the sinnes of all th'earth,
No satisfaction could the world afford:
    But this rich Jewell, which from God was sent,
    To call all those that would in time repent.

Which I present (deare Lady) to your view,
Upon the Crosse depriv'd of life or breath,
To judge if ever Lover were so true,
To yeeld himselfe unto such shamefull death:
Now blessed *Joseph* doth both beg and sue,
To have his body who possest his faith,
    And thinkes, if he this small request obtaines,
    He wins more wealth than in the world remaines.

Thus

Thus honourable *Joseph* is possest,
Of what his heart and soule so much desired,
And now he goes to give that body rest,
That all his life, with griefes and paines was tired;
He finds a Tombe, a Tombe most rarely blest,
In which was never creature yet interred;
    There this most pretious body he incloses,
    Imbalmd and deckt with Lillies and with Roses.

Loe here the Beautie of Heav'n and Earth is laid,
The purest coulers underneath the Sunne,
But in this place he cannot long be staid,
Glory must end what horror hath begun;
For he the furie of the Heavens obay'd,
And now he must possesse what he hath wonne:
    The *Maries* doe with pretious balmes attend,
    But beeing come, they find it to no end.

¶ For he is rize from Death t'Eternall Life, *Christs re-*
And now those pretious oyntments he desires *surrection.*
Are brought unto him, by his faithfull Wife
The holy Church; who in those rich attires,
Of Patience, Love, Long suffring, Voide of strife,
Humbly presents those oyntments he requires:
    The oyles of Mercie, Charitie, and Faith,
    Shee onely gives that which no other hath.

¶ These pretious balmes doe heale his grievous wounds, *A briefe de-*
And water of Compunction washeth cleane *scription of*
The soares of sinnes, which in our Soules abounds; *his beautie*
So faire it heales, no skarre is ever seene; *upon the*
Yet all the glory unto Christ redounds, *Canticles.*
His pretious blood is that which must redeeme;
    Those well may make us lovely in his sight,
    But cannot save without his powrefull might.

This

This is that Bridegroome that appeares so faire,
So sweet, so lovely in his Spouses sight,
That unto Snowe we may his face compare,
His cheekes like skarlet, and his eyes so bright
As purest Doves that in the rivers are,
Washed with milke, to give the more delight;
    His head is likened to the finest gold,
    His curled lockes so beauteous to behold;

Blacke as a Raven in her blackest hew;
His lips like skarlet threeds, yet much more sweet
Than is the sweetest hony dropping dew,
Or hony combes, where all the Bees doe meete;
Yea, he is constant, and his words are true,
His cheekes are beds of spices, flowers sweet;
    His lips like Lillies, dropping downe pure mirrhe,
    Whose love, before all worlds we doe preferre.

To my Lady of Cumber-land.

¶ Ah! give me leave (good Lady) now to leave
This taske of Beauty which I tooke in hand,
I cannot wade so deepe, I may deceave
My selfe, before I can attaine the land;
Therefore (good Madame) in your heart I leave
His perfect picture, where it still shall stand,
    Deepely engraved in that holy shrine,
    Environed with Love and Thoughts divine.

There may you see him as a God in glory,
And as a man in miserable case;
There may you reade his true and perfect storie,
His bleeding body there you may embrace,
And kisse his dying cheekes with teares of sorrow,
With joyfull griefe, you may intreat for grace;
    And all your prayers, and your almes-deeds
    May bring to stop his cruell wounds that bleeds.

Oft

Oft times hath he made triall of your love,
And in your Faith hath tooke no small delight,
By Crosses and Afflictions he doth prove,
Yet still your heart remaineth firme and right;
Your love so strong, as nothing can remove,
Your thoughts beeing placed on him both day and night,
    Your constant soule doth lodge between her brests,
    This Sweet of sweets, in which all glory rests.

Sometime h'appears to thee in Shepheards weed,
And so presents himselfe before thine eyes,
A good old man; that goes his flocke to feed;
Thy colour changes, and thy heart doth rise;
Thou call'st, he comes, thou find'st tis he indeed,
Thy Soule conceaves that he is truely wise:
    Nay more, desires that he may be the Booke,
    Whereon thine eyes continually may looke.

Sometime imprison'd, naked, poore, and bare,
Full of diseases, impotent, and lame,
Blind, deafe, and dumbe, he comes unto his faire,
To see if yet shee will remaine the same;
Nay sicke and wounded, now thou do'st prepare
To cherish him in thy deare Lovers name:
    Yea thou bestow'st all paines, all cost, all care,
    That may relieve him, and his health repaire.

These workes of mercy are so sweete, so deare
To him that is the Lord of Life and Love,
That all thy prayers he vouchsafes to heare,
And sends his holy Spirit from above;
Thy eyes are op'ned, and thou seest so cleare,
No worldly thing can thy faire mind remove;
    Thy faith, thy prayers, and his speciall grace
    Doth open Heav'n, where thou behold'st his face.

These

These are those Keyes Saint *Peter* did possesse,
Which with a spirituall powre are giv'n to thee,
To heale the Soules of those that doe transgresse,
By thy faire virtues; which, if once they see,
Unto the like they doe their minds addresse,
Such as thou art, such they desire to be:
    If they be blind, thou giv'st to them their sight;
    If deafe or lame, they heare, and goe upright.

Yea, if possest with any evill spirits,
Such powre thy faire examples have obtain'd
To cast them out, applying Christs pure merits,
By which they are bound, and of all hurt restrain'd:
If strangely taken, wanting sence or wits,
Thy faith appli'd unto their soules so pain'd,
    Healeth all griefes, and makes them grow so strong,
    As no defects can hang upon them long.

Then beeing thus rich, no riches do'st respect,
Nor do'st thou care for any outward showe;
The proud that doe faire Virtues rules neglect,
Desiring place, thou fittest them belowe:
All wealth and honour thou do'st quite reject,
If thou perceiv'st that once it prooves a foe
    To virtue, learning, and the powres divine,
    Thou mai'st convert, but never wilt incline

To fowle disorder, or licentiousnesse,
But in thy modest vaile do'st sweetly cover
The staines of other sinnes, to make themselves,
That by this means thou mai'st in time recover
Those weake lost sheepe that did so long transgresse,
Presenting them unto thy deerest Lover;
    That when he brings them backe unto his fold,
    In their conversion then he may behold

Thy

Thy beauty shining brighter than the Sunne,
Thine honour more than ever Monarke gaind,
Thy wealth exceeding his that Kingdomes wonne,
Thy Love unto his Spouse, thy Faith unfaind,
Thy Constancy in what thou hast begun,
Till thou his heavenly Kingdom have obtained;
    Respecting worldly wealth to be but drosse,
    Which, if abuz'd, doth proove the owners losse.

Great *Cleopatra's* love to *Anthony,*
Can no way be compared unto thine;
Shee left her Love in his extremitie,
When greatest need should cause her to combine
Her force with his, to get the Victory:
Her Love was earthly, and thy Love Divine;
    Her Love was onely to support her pride,
    Humilitie thy Love and Thee doth guide.

That glorious part of Death, which last shee plai'd,
T'appease the ghost of her deceased Love,
Had never needed, if shee could have stai'd
When his extreames made triall, and did prove
Her leaden love unconstant, and afraid:
Their wicked warres the wrath of God might move
    To take revenge for chast *Octavia's* wrongs,
    Because shee enjoyes what unto her belongs.

No *Cleopatra,* though thou wert as faire
As any Creature in *Antonius* eyes;
Yea though thou wert as rich, as wise, as rare,
As any Pen could write, or Wit devise;
Yet with this Lady canst thou not compare,
Whose inward virtues all thy worth denies:
    Yet though a blacke Egyptian do'st appeare;
    Thou false, shee true; and to her Love more deere.

Shee

Shee sacrificeth to her deerest Love,
With flowres of Faith, and garlands of Good deeds;
Shee flies not from him when afflictions prove,
Shee beares his crosse, and stops his wounds that bleeds;
Shee loves and lives chaste as the Turtle dove,
Shee attends upon him, and his flocke shee feeds;
      Yea for one touch of death which thou did'st trie,
      A thousand deaths shee every day doth die.

Her virtuous life exceeds thy worthy death,
Yea, she hath richer ornaments of state,
Shining more glorious than in dying breath
Thou didst; when either pride, or cruell fate,
Did worke thee to prevent a double death;
To stay the malice, scorne, and cruell hate
      Of Rome; that joy'd to see thy pride pull'd downe,
      Whose Beauty wrought the hazard of her Crowne.

Good Madame, though your modestie be such,
Not to acknowledge what we know and find;
And that you thinke these prayses overmuch,
Which doe expresse the beautie of your mind;
Yet pardon me although I give a touch
Unto their eyes, that else would be so blind,
      As not to see thy store, and their owne wants,
      From whose faire seeds of Virtue spring these plants.

And knowe, when first into this world I came,
This charge was giv'n me by th'Eternall powres,
Th'everlasting Trophie of thy fame,
To build and decke it with the sweetest flowres
That virtue yeelds; Then Madame, doe not blame
Me, when I shew the World but what is yours,
      And decke you with that crowne which is your due,
      That of Heav'ns beauty Earth may take a view.

Though

Though famous women elder times have knowne,
Whose glorious actions did appeare so bright,
That powrefull men by them were overthrowne,
And all their armies overcome in fight;
The Scythian women by their powre alone,
Put king *Darius* unto shamefull flight:
　　All Asia yeelded to their conq'ring hand,
　　Great *Alexander* could not their powre withstand.

Whose worth, though writ in lines of blood and fire,
Is not to be compared unto thine;
Their powre was small to overcome Desire,
Or to direct their wayes by Virtues line:
Were they alive, they would thy Life admire,
And unto thee their honours would resigne:
　　For thou a greater conquest do'st obtaine,
　　Than they who have so many thousands slaine.

Wise *Deborah* that judged Israel,
Nor valiant *Judeth* cannot equall thee,
Unto the first, God did his will reveale,
And gave her powre to set his people free;
Yea *Judeth* had the powre likewise to queale
Proud *Holifernes*, that the just might see
　　What small defence vaine pride, and greatnesse hath
　　Against the weapons of Gods word and faith.

But thou farre greater warre do'st still maintaine,
Against that many headed monster Sinne,
Whose mortall sting hath many thousand slaine,
And every day fresh combates doe begin;
Yet cannot all his venome lay one staine,
Upon thy Soule, thou do'st the conquest winne,
　　Though all the world he daily doth devoure,
　　Yet over thee he never could get powre.

For

For that one worthy deed by *Deb'rah* done,
Thou hast performed many in thy time;
For that one Conquest that faire *Judeth* wonne,
By which shee did the steps of honour clime,
Thou hast the Conquest of all Conquests wonne,
When to thy Conscience Hell can lay no crime:
    For that one head that *Judeth* bare away,
    Thou tak'st from Sinne a hundred heads a day.

Though virtuous *Hester* fasted three dayes space,
And spent her time in prayers all that while,
That by Gods powre shee might obtaine such grace,
That shee and hers might not become a spoyle
To wicked *Hamon*, in whose crabbed face
Was seene the map of malice, envie, guile;
    Her glorious garments though shee put apart,
    So to present a pure and single heart

To God, in sack-cloth, ashes, and with teares;
Yet must faire *Hester* needs give place to thee,
Who hath continu'd dayes, weekes, months, and yeares,
In Gods true service, yet thy heart beeing free
From doubt of death, or any other feares:
Fasting from sinne, thou pray'st thine eyes may see
    Him that hath full possession of thine heart,
    From whose sweet love thy Soule can never part.

His Love, not Feare, makes thee to fast and pray,
No kinsmans counsell needs thee to advise;
The sack-cloth thou do'st weare both night and day,
Is worldly troubles, which thy rest denies;
The ashes are the Vanities that play
Over thy head, and steale before thine eyes;
    Which thou shak'st off when mourning time is past,
    That royall roabes thou may'st put on at last.

Joachims

Joachims wife, that faire and constant Dame,
Who rather chose a cruel death to die,
Than yeeld to those two Elders voide of shame,
When both at once her chastitie did trie,
Whose Innocencie bare away the blame,
Untill th'Almighty Lord had heard her crie;
    And rais'd the spirit of a Child to speake,
    Making the powrefull judged of the weake.

Although her virtue doe deserve to be
Writ by that hand that never purchas'd blame;
In holy Writ, where all the world may see
Her perfit life, and ever honoured name:
Yet was she not to be compar'd to thee,
Whose many virtues doe increase thy fame:
    For shee oppos'd against old doting Lust,
    Who with lifes danger she did feare to trust.

But your chaste breast, guarded with strength of mind,
Hates the imbracements of unchaste desires;
You loving God, live in your selfe confind
From unpure Love, your purest thoughts retires,
Your perfit sight could never be so blind,
To entertaine the old or yong desires
    Of idle Lovers; which the world presents,
    Whose base abuses worthy minds prevents.

Even as the constant Lawrell, always greene,
No parching heate of Summer can deface,
Nor pinching Winter ever yet was seene,
Whose nipping frists could wither, or disgrace:
So you (deere Ladie) still remaine as Queene,
Subduing all affections that are base,
    Unalterable by the change of times,
    Not following, but lamenting others crimes.

No

No feare of Death, or dread of open shame,
Hinders your perfect heart to give consent;
Nor loathsome age, whom Time could never tame
From ill designes, whereto their youth was bent;
But love of God, care to preserve your fame,
And spend that pretious time that God hath sent,
  In all good exercises of the minde,
  Whereto your noble nature is inclin'd.

That Ethyopian Queene did gaine great fame,
Who from the Southerne world, did come to see
Great *Salomon*; the glory of whose name
Had spread it selfe ore all the earth, to be
So great, that all the Princes thither came,
To be spectators of his royaltie:
  And this faire Queene of Sheba came from farre,
  To reverence this new appearing starre.

From th'utmost part of all the Earth shee came,
To heare the Wisdom of this worthy King;
To trie if Wonder did agree with Fame,
And many faire rich presents did she bring:
Yea many strange hard questions did shee frame,
All which were answer'd by this famous King:
  Nothing was hid that in her heart did rest,
  And all to proove this King so highly blest.

Here Majestie with Majestie did meete,
Wisdome to Wisdome yeelded true content,
One Beauty did another Beauty greet,
Bounty to Bountie never could repent;
Here all distaste is troden under feet,
No losse of time, where time was so well spent
  In vertuous exercises of the minde,
  In which this Queene did much contentment finde.

Spirits

Spirits affect where they doe sympathize,
Wisdom desires Wisdome to embrace,
Virtue covets her like, and doth devize
How she her friends may entertaine with grace;
Beauty sometime is pleas'd to feed her eyes,
With viewing Beautie in anothers face:
    Both good and bad in this point doe agree,
    That each desireth with his like to be.

And this Desire did worke a strange effect,
To drawe a Queene forth of her native Land,
Not yeelding to the nicenesse and respect
Of woman-kind; shee past both sea and land,
All feare of dangers shee did quite neglect,
Onely to see, to heare, and understand
    That beauty, wisedome, majestie, and glorie,
    That in her heart imprest his perfect storie.

Yet this faire map of majestie and might,
Was but a figure of thy deerest Love,
Borne t'expresse that true and heavenly light,
That doth all other joyes imperfect prove;
If this faire Earthly starre did shine so bright,
What doth that glorious Sonne that is above?
    Who weares th'imperiall crowne of heaven and earth,
    And made all Christians blessed in his berth.

If that small sparke could yeeld so great a fire,
As to inflame the hearts of many Kings
To come to see, to heare, and to admire
His wisdome, tending but to worldly things;
Then much more reason have we to desire
That heav'nly wisedome, which salvation brings;
    The Sonne of righteousnesse, that gives true joyes,
    When all they sought for, were but Earthly toyes.

No

No travels ought th'affected soule to shunne,
That the faire heavenly Light desires to see:
This King of kings to whom we all should runne,
To view his Glory and his Majestie;
He without whom we all had been undone,
He that from Sinne and Death hath set us free,
    And overcome Satan, the world, and sinne,
    That by his merits we those joyes might winne.

Prepar'd by him, whose everlasting throne
Is plac'd in heaven, above the starrie skies,
Where he that sate, was like the Jasper stone,
Who rightly knowes him shall he truely wise,
A Rainebow round about his glorious throne;
Nay more, those winged beasts so full of eies,
    That never cease to glorifie his Name,
    Who was, and will be, and is now the same.

This is that great almightie Lord that made
Both heaven and earth, and lives for evermore;
By him the worlds foundation first was laid:
He fram'd the things that never were before:
The Sea within his bounds by him is staid,
He judgeth all alike, both rich and poore:
    All might, all majestie, all love, all lawe
    Remaines in him that keepes all worlds in awe.

From his eternall throne the lightning came,
Thundrings and Voyces did from thence proceede;
And all the creatures glorifi'd his name,
In heaven, in earth, and seas, they all agreed,
When loe that spotlesse Lambe so voyd of blame,
That for us di'd, whose sinnes did make him bleed:
    That true Physition that so many heales,
    Opened the Booke, and did undoe the Seales.

He

He onely worthy to undoe the Booke
Of our charg'd soules, full of iniquitie,
Where with the eyes of mercy he doth looke
Upon our weakenesse and infirmitie;
This is that corner stone that was forsooke,
Who leaves it, trusts but to uncertaintie:
    This is Gods Sonne, in whom he is well pleased,
    His deere beloved, that his wrath appeased.

He that had powre to open all the Seales,
And summon up our sinnes of blood and wrong,
He unto whom the righteous soules appeales,
That have bin martyrd, and doe thinke it long,
To whom in mercie he his will reveales,
That they should rest a little in their wrong,
    Untill their fellow servants should be killed,
    Even as they were, and that they were fulfilled.

¶ Pure thoughted Lady, blessed be thy choice
Of this Almightie, everlasting King;
In thee his Saints and Angels doe rejoyce,
And to their Heav'nly Lord doe daily sing
Thy perfect praises in their lowdest voyce;
And all their harpes and golden vials bring
    Full of sweet odours, even thy holy prayers
    Unto that spotlesse Lambe, that all repaires.

To the Lady dowager of Cumberland.

Of whom that Heathen Queene obtain'd such grace,
By honouring but the shadow of his Love,
That great Judiciall day to have a place,
Condemning those that doe unfaithfull prove;
Among the haplesse, happie is her case,
That her deere Saviour spake for her behove;
    And that her memorable Act should be
    Writ by the hand of true Eternitie.

Yet

Yet this rare Phoenix of that worne-out age,
This great majesticke Queene comes short of thee,
Who to an earthly Prince did then ingage
Her hearts desires, her love, her libertie,
Acting her glorious part upon a Stage
Of weaknesse, frailtie, and infirmity :
    Giving all honour to a Creature, due
    To her Creator, whom shee never knew.

But loe, a greater thou hast sought and found
Than *Salomon* in all his royaltie ;
And unto him thy faith most firmely bound
To serve and honour him continually ;
That glorious God, whose terror doth confound
All sinfull workers of iniquitie :
    Him hast thou truely served all thy life,
    And for his love, liv'd with the world at strife.

To this great Lord, thou onely art affected,
Yet came he not in pompe or royaltie,
But in an humble habit, base, dejected ;
A King, a God, clad in mortalitie,
He hath thy love, thou art by him directed,
His perfect path was faire humilitie :
    Who being Monarke of heav'n, earth, and seas,
    Indur'd all wrongs, yet no man did displease.

Then how much more art thou to be commended,
That seek'st thy love in lowly shepheards weed?
A seeming Trades-mans sonne, of none attended,
Save of a few in povertie and need ;
Poore Fishermen that on his love attended,
His love that makes so many thousands bleed :
    Thus did he come, to trie our faiths the more,
    Possessing worlds, yet seeming extreame poore.

The

The Pilgrimes travels, and the Shepheards cares,
He tooke upon him to enlarge our soules,
What pride hath lost, humilitie repaires,
For by his glorious death he us inroules
In deepe Characters, writ with blood and teares,
Upon those blessed Everlasting scroules;
  His hands, his feete, his body, and his face,
  Whence freely flow'd the rivers of his grace.

Sweet holy rivers, pure celestiall springs,
Proceeding from the fountaine of our life;
Swift sugred currents that salvation brings,
Cleare chrystall streames, purging all sinne and strife,
Faire floods, where souls do bathe their snow-white wings,
Before they flie to true eternall life:
  Sweet Nectar and Ambrosia, food of Saints,
  Which, whoso tasteth, never after faints.

This hony dropping due of holy love,
Sweet milke, wherewith we weaklings are restored,
Who drinkes thereof, a world can never move,
All earthly pleasures are of them abhorred;
This love made Martyrs many deaths to prove,
To taste his sweetnesse, whom they so adored:
  Sweetnesse that makes our flesh a burthen to us,
  Knowing it serves but onely to undoe us.

His sweetnesse sweet'ned all the sowre of death,
To faithfull *Stephen* his appointed Saint;
Who by the river stones did loose his breath,
When paines nor terrors could not make him faint:
So was this blessed Martyr turn'd to earth,
To glorifie his soule by deaths attaint:
  This holy Saint was humbled and cast downe,
  To winne in heaven an everlasting crowne.

Whose

Whose face repleat with Majestie and Sweetnesse,
Did as an Angel unto them appeare,
That sate in Counsell hearing his discreetnesse,
Seeing no change, or any signe of a feare;
But with a constant browe did there confesse
Christs high deserts, which were to him so deare:
    Yea when these Tyrants stormes did most oppresse,
    Christ did appeare to make his griefe the lesse.

For beeing filled with the holy Ghost,
Up unto Heav'n he look'd with stedfast eies,
Where God appeared with his heavenly hoste
In glory to this Saint before he dies;
Although he could no Earthly pleasures boast,
At Gods right hand sweet JESUS he espies;
    Bids them behold Heavens open, he doth see
    The Sonne of Man at Gods right hand to be.

Whose sweetnesse sweet'ned that short sowre of Life,
Making all bitternesse delight his taste,
Yeelding sweet quietnesse in bitter strife,
And most contentment when he di'd disgrac'd;
Heaping up joyes where sorrows were most rife;
Such sweetnesse could not choose but be imbrac'd:
    The food of Soules, the Spirits onely treasure,
    The Paradise of our celestiall pleasure.

This Lambe of God, who di'd, and was alive,
Presenting us the bread of life Eternall,
His bruised body powrefull to revive
Our sinking soules, out of the pit infernall;
For by this blessed food he did contrive
A worke of grace, by this his gift externall,
    With heav'nly Manna, food of his elected,
    To feed their soules, of whom he is respected.

This

This, wheate of Heaven the blessed Angells bread,
Wherewith he feedes his deere adopted Heires;
Sweet foode of life that doth revive the dead,
And from the living takes away all cares;
To taste this sweet Saint *Laurence* did not dread,
The broyling gridyrone cool'd with holy teares:
    Yeelding his naked body to the fire,
    To taste this sweetnesse, such was his desire.

Nay, what great sweetnesse did th'Apostles taste,
Condemn'd by Counsell, when they did returne;
Rejoycing that for him they di'd disgrac'd,
Whose sweetnes made their hearts and soules so burne
With holy Zeale and love most pure and chaste;
For him they sought from whome they might not turne:
    Whose love made *Andrew* goe most joyfully,
    Unto the Crosse, on which he meant to die.

The Princes of th'Apostles were so filled
With the delicious sweetnes of his grace,
That willingly they yeelded to be killed,
Receiving deaths that were most vile and base,
For his name sake, that all might be fulfilled.
They with great joy all torments did imbrace:
    The ugli'st face that Death could ever yeeld,
    Could never feare these Champions from the field.

They still continued in their glorious fight,
Against the enemies of flesh and blood;
And in Gods law did set their whole delight,
Suppressing evill, and erecting good:
Not sparing Kings in what they did not right;
Their noble Actes they seal'd with deerest blood:
    One chose the Gallowes, that unseemely death,
    The other by the Sword did loose his breath.

His

His Head did pay the dearest rate of sin,
Yeelding it joyfully unto the Sword,
To be cut off as he had never bin,
For speaking truth according to Gods word,
Telling king *Herod* of incestuous sin,
That hatefull crime of God and man abhorr'd:
> His brothers wife, that prowd licentious Dame,
> Cut off his Head to take away his shame.

Loe Madame, heere you take a view of those,
Whose worthy steps you doe desire to tread,
Deckt in those colours which our Saviour chose;
Colours of   The purest colours both of White and Red,
Confessors   Their freshest beauties would I faine disclose,
and Martirs.   By which our Saviour most was honoured:
> But my weake Muse desireth now to rest,
> Folding up all their Beauties in your breast.

Whose excellence hath rais'd my sprites to write,
Of what my thoughts could hardly apprehend;
Your rarest Virtues did my soule delight,
Great Ladie of my heart: I must commend
You that appeare so faire in all mens sight:
On your Deserts my Muses doe attend:
> You are the Articke Starre that guides my hand,
> All what I am, I rest at your command.

FINIS

The Description of Cooke-ham

Farewell (sweet Cooke-ham) where I first obtain'd
Grace from that Grace where perfit Grace remain'd;
And where the Muses gave their full consent,
I should have powre the virtuous to content:
Where princely Palace will'd me to indite,
The sacred Storie of the Soules delight.
Farewell (sweet Place) where Virtue then did rest,
And all delights did harbour in her breast:
Never shall my sad eies againe behold
Those pleasures which my thoughts did then unfold:
Yet you (great Lady) Mistris of that Place,
From whose desires did spring this worke of Grace;
Vouchsafe to thinke upon those pleasures past,
As fleeting worldly Joyes that could not last:
Or, as dimme shadowes of celestiall pleasures,
Which are desir'd above all earthly treasures.
Oh how (me thought) against you thither came,
Each part did seeme some new delight to frame!
The House receiv'd all ornaments to grace it,
And would indure no foulenesse to deface it.
The Walkes put on their summer Liveries,
And all things else did hold like similies:
The Trees with leaves, with fruits, with flowers clad,
Embrac'd each other, seeming to be glad,
Turning themselves to beauteous Canopies,
To shade the bright Sunne from your brighter eies:
The cristall Streames with silver spangles graced,

While

While by the glorious Sunne they were embraced:
The little Birds in chirping notes did sing,
To entertaine both You and that sweet Spring.
And *Philomela* with her sundry leyes,
Both You and that delightfull Place did praise.
Oh how me thought each plant, each floure, each tree
Set forth their beauties then to welcome thee:
The very Hills right humbly did descend,
When you to tread upon them did intend.
And as you set your feete, they still did rise,
Glad that they could receive so rich a prize.
The gentle Windes did take delight to bee
Among those woods that were so grac'd by thee.
And in sad murmure utterd pleasing sound,
That Pleasure in that place might more abound:
The swelling Bankes deliver'd all their pride,
When such a *Phoenix* once they had espide.
Each Arbor, Banke, each Seate, each stately Tree,
Thought themselves honor'd in supporting thee.
The pretty Birds would oft come to attend thee,
Yet flie away for feare they should offend thee:
The little creatures in the Burrough by
Would come abroad to sport them in your eye;
Yet fearefull of the Bowe in your faire Hand,
Would runne away when you did make a stand.
Now let me come unto that stately Tree,
Wherein such goodly prospects you did see;
That Oake that did in height his fellowes passe,
As much as lofty trees, low growing grasse:
Much like a comely Cedar streight and tall,
Whose beauteous stature farre exceeded all:
How often did you visite this faire tree,
Which seeming joyfull in receiving thee,
Would like a Palme tree spread his armes abroad,

Desirous

Desirous that you there should make abode:
Whose faire greene leaves much like a comely vaile,
Defended *Phebus* when he would assaile:
Whose pleasing boughes did yeeld a coole fresh ayre,
Joying his happinesse when you were there.
Where beeing seated, you might plainely see,
Hills, vales, and woods, as if on bended knee
They had appeard, your honour to salute,
Or to preferre some strange unlook'd for sute:
All interlac'd with brookes and christall springs,
A Prospect fit to please the eyes of Kings:
And thirteene shires appear'd all in your sight,
Europe could not affoard much more delight.
What was there then but gave you all content,
While you the time in meditation spent,
Of their Creators powre, which there you saw,
In all his Creatures held a perfit Law;
And in their beauties did you plaine descrie,
His beauty, wisdome, grace, love, majestie.
In these sweet woods how often did you walke,
With Christ and his Apostles there to talke;
Placing his holy Writ in some faire tree,
To meditate what you therein did see:
With *Moyses* you did mount his holy Hill,
To know his pleasure, and performe his Will.
With lovely *David* you did often sing,
His holy Hymnes to Heavens Eternall King.
And in sweet musicke did your soule delight,
To sound his prayses, morning, noone, and night.
With blessed *Joseph* you did often feed
Your pined brethren, when they stood in need.
And that sweet Lady sprung from *Cliffords* race,
Of noble *Bedfords* blood, faire streame of Grace;
To honourable *Dorset* now espows'd,

In

In whose faire breast true virtue then was hous'd:
Oh what delight did my weake spirits find
In those pure parts of her well framed mind:
And yet it grieves me that I cannot be
Neere unto her, whose virtues did agree
With those faire ornaments of outward beauty,
Which did enforce from all both love and dutie.
Unconstant Fortune, thou art most too blame,
Who casts us downe into so lowe a frame:
Where our great friends we cannot dayly see,
So great a diffrence is there in degree.
Many are placed in those Orbes of state,
Parters in honour, so ordain'd by Fate;
Neerer in show, yet farther off in love,
In which, the lowest alwayes are above.
But whither am I carried in conceit?
My Wit too weake to conster of the great.
Why not? although we are but borne of earth,
We may behold the Heavens, despising death;
And loving heaven that is so farre above,
May in the end vouchsafe us entire love.
Therefore sweet Memorie doe thou retaine
Those pleasures past, which will not turne againe;
Remember beauteous *Dorsets* former sports,
So farre from beeing toucht by ill reports;
Wherein my selfe did alwaies beare a part,
While reverend Love presented my true heart:
Those recreations let me beare in mind,
Which her sweet youth and noble thoughts did finde:
Whereof depriv'd, I evermore must grieve,
Hating blind Fortune, carelesse to relieve.
And you sweet Cooke-ham, whom these Ladies leave,
I now must tell the griefe you did conceave
At their departure; when they went away,

How

How every thing retaind a sad dismay:
Nay long before, when once an inkeling came,
Me thought each thing did unto sorrow frame:
The trees that were so glorious in our view,
Forsooke both floures and fruit, when once they knew
Of your depart, their very leaves did wither,
Changing their colours as they grewe together.
But when they saw this had no powre to stay you,
They often wept, though speechlesse, could not pray you;
Letting their teares in your faire bosoms fall,
As if they said, Why will ye leave us all?
This being vaine, they cast their leaves away,
Hoping that pitie would have made you stay:
Their frozen tops, like Ages hoarie haires,
Showes their disasters, languishing in feares:
A swarthy riveld ryne all over spread,
Their dying bodies halfe alive, halfe dead.
But your occasions call'd you so away,
That nothing there had power to make you stay:
Yet did I see, a noble gratefull minde,
Requiting each according to their kind,
Forgetting not to turne and take your leave
Of these sad creatures, powrelesse to receive
Your favour, when with griefe you did depart,
Placing their former pleasures in your heart;
Giving great charge to noble Memory,
There to preserve their love continually:
But specially the love of that faire tree,
That first and last you did vouchsafe to see:
In which it pleas'd you oft to take the ayre,
With noble *Dorset*, then a virgin faire:
Where many a learned Booke was read and skand
To this faire tree, taking me by the hand,
You did repeat the pleasures which had past,

Seeming

Seeming to grieve they could no longer last.
And with a chaste, yet loving kisse took leave,
Of which sweet kisse I did it soone bereave:
Scorning a sencelesse creature should possesse
So rare a favour, so great happinesse.
No other kisse it could receive from me,
For feare to give backe what it tooke of thee:
So I ingratefull Creature did deceive it,
Of that which you vouchsaft in love to leave it.
And though it oft had giv'n me much content,
Yet this great wrong I never could repent:
But of the happiest made it most forlorne,
To shew that nothing's free from Fortunes scorne,
While all the rest with this most beauteous tree,
Made their sad consort Sorrowes harmony.
The Flowres that on the banks and walkes did grow,
Crept in the ground, the Grasse did weepe for woe.
The Windes and Waters seem'd to chide together,
Because you went away they knew not whither:
And those sweet Brookes that ran so faire and cleare,
With griefe and trouble wrinckled did appeare.
Those pretty Birds that wonted were to sing,
Now neither sing, nor chirp, nor use their wing;
But with their tender feet on some bare spray,
Warble forth sorrow, and their owne dismay.
Faire *Philomela* leaves her mournefull Ditty,
Drownd in dead sleepe, yet can procure no pittie:
Each arbour, banke, each seate, each stately tree,
Lookes bare and desolate now for want of thee;
Turning greene tresses into frostie gray,
While in cold griefe they wither all away.
The Sunne grew weake, his beames no comfort gave,
While all greene things did make the earth their grave:
Each brier, each bramble, when you went away,

Caugh

Caught fast your clothes, thinking to make you stay:
Delightfull Eccho wonted to reply
To our last words, did now for sorrow die:
The house cast off each garment that might grace it,
Putting on Dust and Cobwebs to deface it.
All desolation then there did appeare,
When you were going whom they held so deare.
This last farewell to *Cooke-ham* here I give,
When I am dead thy name in this may live,
Wherein I have perform'd her noble hest,
Whose virtues lodge in my unworthy breast,
And ever shall, so long as life remaines,
Tying my heart to her by those rich chaines.

FINIS

To the Doubtfull Reader

Gentle Reader, if thou desire to be resolved, why I give this title, *Salve Deus Rex Judæorum*, know for certaine that it was delivered unto me in sleepe many yeares before I had any intent to write in this maner, and was quite out of my memory, until I had written the Passion of Christ, when immediately it came into my remembrance, what I had dreamed long before; and thinking it a significant token, that I was appointed to performe this Worke, I gave the very same words I received in sleepe as the fittest title I could devise for this Booke.